GLADWYNE FREE LIBRARY

W9-BML-900

Knit Fix

Problem Solving for Knitters

Lisa Kartus

INTERWEAVE PRESS
www.interweave.com

Design: Rebecca Finkel
Photography: Joe Coca

Text © 2006, Lisa Kartus
Photography © 2006, Interweave Press LLC

All rights reserved.

Interweave Press LLC
201 East Fourth Street
Loveland, CO 80537-5655 USA
www.interweave.com

Printed in China through Asia Pacific Offset

Library of Congress Cataloging-in-Publication Data

Kartus, Lisa, 1953-
   Knit fix : problem solving for knitters / Lisa Kartus,
author.
      p. cm.
   Includes index.
   ISBN-13: 978-1-59668-011-1 (hardbound)
   ISBN-10: 1-59668-011-3 (hardbound)
1. Knitting. I. Title.
   TT820.K33 2006
   746.43'2--dc22

                              2006002416

10 9 8 7 6 5 4 3 2 1

Contents

Introduction 4

chapter 1
Your Knitting Philosophy 7

chapter 2
Knitting Foundations 11

chapter 3
Fixes You'll Use Again and Again 19

chapter 4
Troubleshooting 25

chapter 5
**Solving Problems
Before They Grow** 51

chapter 6
**Extreme Fixes: Altering When
You're Done Knitting** 75

chapter 7
Test-Driving 87

Conclusion 105

Acknowledgments 107

The Basics of Knitting 108

A Guide to Common Errors 109

Index 110

Introduction

*O**ne of the many things that I learned from my father-in-law was that it was all right to make mistakes. Dr. Irving Kartus was a Freudian psychiatrist with a sense of humor and a strong grip on reality. He carried a key ring with a rectangular brass medallion that read "nearly normal."***

Humans at their best are nearly normal. No one's perfect. Mistakes happen. Learn. Then move on. It's a forgiving attitude, one that took me a while to adopt, but that eventually brought calm into my life.

I took up knitting as an adult in the mid-1980s. At the time I was a freelance writer covering finance, and I often found myself sitting through long meetings, the sort attended by a hundred people. Rather than sneaking looks at my watch, I thought it would be nice to have something to do with my hands. One day, I stopped by the local yarn store before catching the train to Chicago from my suburban home. There I bought a sweater pattern, yarn, and needles.

Like most girls in the 1960s, I'd learned the basics of knitting. Evidently what my mother taught me had stuck. Twenty-five years later, before I left

that yarn store with my eight skeins of pink cotton, I said to the owner, "Now remind me. To purl, I throw the yarn in front, right?"

At the meeting downtown, I cast on and knitted at every opportunity. With my hands busy, my brain absorbed every word uttered by every chief executive officer. Friends and co-workers couldn't believe I knit. As I asked those CEOs questions that left them squirming, I broke every stereotype of the grandmotherly knitter.

When I finished the sweater, the bottom ribbing was too tight. I took it to my cousin Shirley, an expert knitter who lived a few towns away. She showed me how to rip out the ribbing and knit it the right size. Then she said, "Now I want to teach you a better way to cast on."

"Couldn't you have shown me that before I started?" I asked, illogically.

"It's never too late."

If Irv taught me it was merely human to make mistakes, it was Shirley who taught me it was possible to fix them. In my knitting I could try anything. If it didn't work, the worst case meant unraveling what I'd made and using the yarn in another project. I became addicted to knitting because I could solve any problem.

Now it's your turn. Want to know why your stitches magically increase when you don't want them to? Want to know how to fix it? Want to know how to fix that knit stitch that should be a purl? Want to know how to change colors of yarn so the giant poppy you're knitting in four shades of red doesn't look puckered and about to wilt? Need answers to all those questions that you were afraid were too silly to ask at the yarn store or of your cousin? In knitting as in life, there is no such thing as a silly question. Just promise me you'll take that first risk and try to fix your mistakes yourself. Don't worry about dropping a stitch—there's a guide for correcting that problem, too. Stick with me. You can do this. In no time, I'll have you knitting in the middle of the night, when your local yarn store is closed, and your cousin is asleep.

chapter 1
Your Knitting Philosophy

*T*here's a learning curve to knitting. At first, we're just happy to make stitches. Then we want those stitches to look neat and even. Then we want them to be the right size so the next sweater actually fits. We constantly expect more from our knitting abilities.

Here's where my father-in-law's "nearly normal" outlook comes in. Say you're at the level of neat stitches doing what you want them to do. The pullover pattern you happen to be following calls for seven rows of garter stitch (knit each stitch in each row) for the hem. You realize five inches past that border that you put in nine rows of garter, not the specified seven. Do you fix it?

Or perhaps you're making a cabled vest and discover that there's a purl stitch where there ought to be a knit. The purl peeks out from behind a cable, so coy that you only noticed it after you'd crossed several more cables (Figure 1).

Do you fix it?

Figure 1: Mistake in cable

General rules to keep you sane

1 In case of brain freeze, ringing phones, demanding family members, or cats suddenly running off with the ball of yarn, remember that the working yarn is your friend. The working yarn—the yarn that runs from your needle to the ball—is attached to the last stitch you made. That last stitch worked should be the stitch closest to the tip of your right needle (Figure 2).

Figure 2: Working yarn

When you return to your knitting from life's interruptions, find the working yarn, make sure you're holding the needle with the last stitch worked in your right hand, and away you go.

2 When you're casting on stitches for anything bigger than a scarf, it helps to place a stitch marker every, say, twenty-five or fifty stitches. If you know you have exactly twenty-five

If you're yelling "of course" right about now, your knitting philosophy is "the pattern is always right." That's fine.

But let me ask, why? Whose sweater is it, anyhow?

How do you decide to fix a mistake?

In my garter hem example, if it's the back of the sweater and you haven't done the front, and if nine rows look fine, just make sure the front matches. But if you've done the back following the pattern's seven rows of garter and it's the front with nine rows, you've got a choice to make.

I have to admit, if I were only five inches past those extra garter rows, I'd probably fix this one because I like fronts and backs to match. But maybe not. What's the real difference in look between nine garter rows and seven? One garter ridge on the right side of the sweater. Do you think anyone will notice? Would anyone notice the peeking purl in the cable? If they do, would you mind? Now you're on your way to a knitting philosophy.

Add in one more thing: Lots of mistakes turn into interesting design possibilities. Say that cable pattern calls for front crosses and you discover you've

stitches before each marker, then counting to make sure you have the correct number of stitches needed is a cinch. Try this, because it's just amazing how often life interrupts when you're counting stitches.

3 When you run across something unfamiliar in a knitting pattern, go ahead and try it anyway. Knitting instructions, like so much in life, make more sense *after* you've tried the technique once. Don't be afraid of messing up. In this book you'll find guidance on translating the instruction and fixing what you've done if it turns out to be the wrong thing.

4 If you're working from a chart, it helps to make an enlarged copy. Also invest in a magnetic board with long rubberized magnet strips, available at knitting or needlework stores. The strips hold your chart in place and mark the exact row you're working.

5 Never fight with your stitches. If you're struggling to move a stitch on the needle or put a needle into a stitch, you're knitting too tightly. Loosen up. This is knitting, not nuclear physics. Or even thumb wrestling.

6 Whatever you do in knitting, do it consistently. Chances are if you've made the same mistake consistently all the way through a project it will look fine.

crossed one in back. Instead of a cable cross there's a swoop (Figure 3).

Think of what would happen if the cable swooped consistently, every few crosses—a modern take on the cable. If, on the other hand, what you want is a classic fisherman sweater, then it's time to fix that cable.

One of the things I love about knitting is that *it's mine*. I can be as picky about it as I want.

Here's my rule: I'll tell you when to panic. Otherwise, don't.

Figure 3: Uncrossed cable

chapter 2
Knitting Foundations

*T*here are only two basic stitches. Like those spies in the movies who synchronize their watches, we'll synchronize stitches.

Let me introduce you to the stitches on your needle (Figures 1 and 2).

Every stitch, knit or purl, has a right leg and a left leg as you look at it. The front leg faces you, the back leg is away from you.

Whether you hold the working yarn in your right hand (English style) or left hand (Continental style), there are four steps each to making a knit or purl stitch.

Figure 1: These are knit stitches.

Right-leg rule

Every stitch, knit and purl, has a front leg and a back leg. Every stitch should sit on the needle with its right leg in front of the needle. Think *right leg forward*. If you knit or purl a stitch with its left leg perched in front of the needle, the stitch will be twisted.

Figure 2: These are purl stitches.

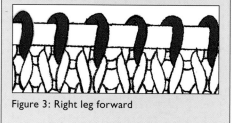

Figure 3: Right leg forward

Knit Stitch

1 With the working yarn under and in back of the needle, place the tip of your right needle between the front and back legs of the first stitch on the left needle (Figures 4 and 5). The tip of the needle points away from you.

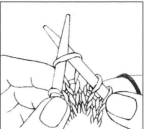
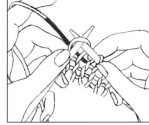

Figure 4: English method   Figure 5: Continental method

2 Wrap the working yarn counter-clockwise around the right needle, the one you just put through the stitch (Figures 6 and 7).

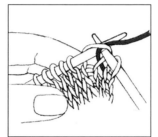

Figure 6: English method   Figure 7: Continental method

3 Pull the right needle back just enough to slip underneath the left needle and pull a new stitch along with it, through the old stitch on the left needle (Figures 8 and 9). (If you're having trouble grabbing hold of the stitch, see Tension on page 16.)

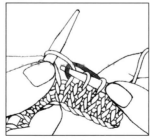
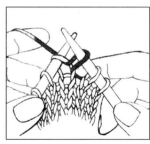

Figure 8: English method   Figure 9: Continental method

4 Slip the old stitch off the left needle (Figures 10 and 11).

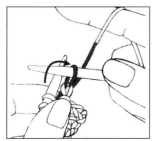

Figure 10: English method   Figure 11: Continental method

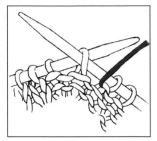

Figure 12: English method

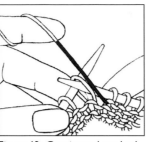

Figure 13: Continental method

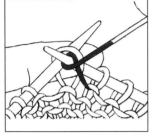

Figure 14: English method

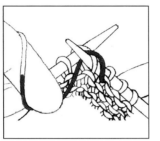

Figure 15: Continental method

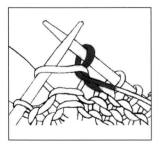

Figure 16: English method

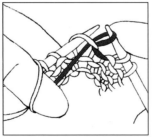

Figure 17: Continental method

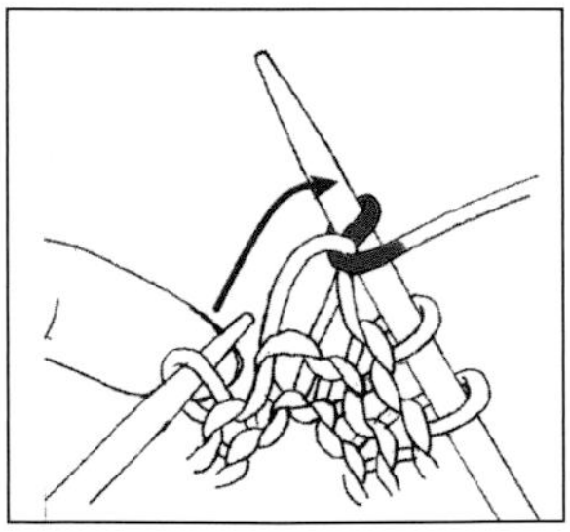

Figure 18: English method

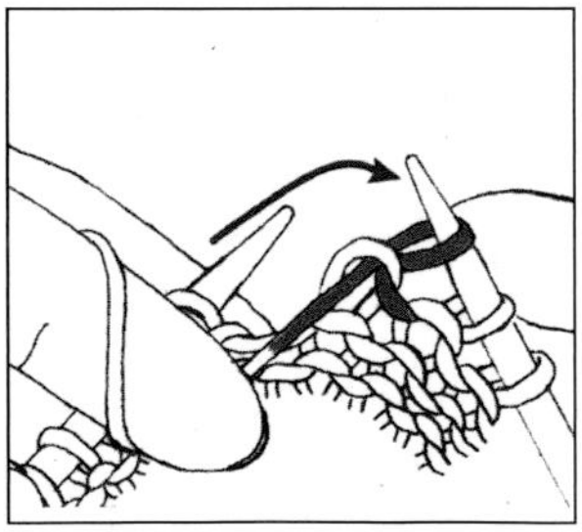

Figure 19: Continental method

Purl Stitch

1 Holding your working yarn to the front, place your right needle between the front and back legs of the first stitch on the left needle from back to front (Figures 12 and 13). This time the tip of the needle points toward you.

2 Wrap the working yarn counter-clockwise around the right needle (Figures 14 and 15).

3 Pull right needle back out of the old stitch and pull the new stitch through (Figures 16 and 17).

4 Slip the old stitch off the left needle (Figures 18 and 19).

A knit stitch that's done correctly looks like this (Figure 20):

A purl stitch that's done correctly looks like this (Figure 21):

Compare them. The knit stitch looks like a V. It feels flat and smooth to the touch. The purl stitch looks like a grain of rice or a seed pearl. Run your finger over the purl stitch and feel the bump. The back of every knit stitch is a purl stitch, and vice versa—whether you're knitting or purling is simply a matter of whether you want that flat knit V or the purl bump on the side of the piece that is facing you.

Figure 20: Knit stitch

Figure 21: Purl stitch

Tension

For some reason, tension remains the too-often-unexplained mystery of knitting. Yet it is simply taking control of the yarn with your hand. Pretty stitches require tension. Part of the mystery is that your hand is doing two things at once—slowing yarn as it comes off the ball and guiding yarn around the needle. Sounds complicated, but it's not. Why? Because there's no wrong way to do it, except to not do it at all. Once your hand acquires muscle memory of holding tension, you'll do it without thinking.

A Few Ways to Hold Tension

1 Okay, this is the way I do it, but don't ask me why. It's just what feels right. When I pick up my knitting, I run the yarn in that crease at the base of my ring finger and my little finger, holding my fingertips to my palm. Then I hook my index finger under the yarn (Figure 22)—this is how I steer yarn around needles and through stitches.

The two best Continental knitters I know hold yarn tension in a similar way, wrapping the yarn twice around the index finger (Figure 23).

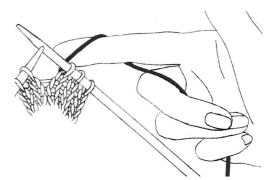

Figure 22: Tension for English method

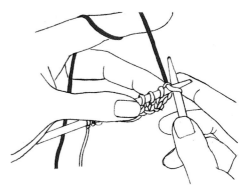

Figure 23: Tension for Continental method

2 VARIATION: Some wonderful knitters hold the yarn between their palms and middle, ring, and little fingers in a fist, then pinch it between thumb and forefinger to guide it (Figure 24).

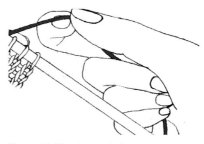

Figure 24: Tension variation

3 VARIATION: Wrap the yarn around the little finger, under the middle and ring fingers, and around the first finger (Figure 25). This is another tension method that will work for both English and Continental knitters.

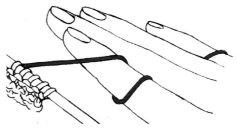

Figure 25: Tension variation

WHAT DOESN'T WORK: holding the yarn between thumb and forefinger to tension and guide the yarn at the same time (Figure 26). The trouble is that it provides irregular tension because you drop the yarn at each stitch.

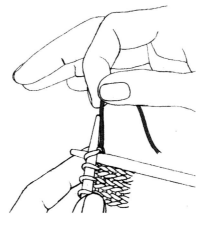

Figure 26: Insufficient tension

chapter 3
Fixes You'll Use Again and Again

*T*hat first pink cotton sweater had a simple design of purl stitches dotted throughout what was otherwise plain stockinette stitch. My husband would point out to friends that I was making all those mistakes—he meant the purls—on purpose. In fact, I was knitting very, very carefully because any mistake would mean a forty-mile trip to see Shirley. My second sweater, though, was an intarsia pattern of flowers, done in about twelve colors. After I'd ripped out the bottom of the back for a third time and started over, it occurred to me that perhaps I could find a way to undo stitches one by one rather than ripping the whole mess out. That's when I figured out how to unknit. At the time I thought I'd invented the technique.

In this section you'll find fixes you'll use again and again: basic repair techniques, one or more of which apply to most knitting problems. I discovered that I tend to make the same handful of mistakes. Now my knitting students find that they, too, have a few errors that are their very own. Consider this section your basic toolbox.

One of my students says that it's when you learn to do the following three maneuvers that you actually start *real* knitting. They're the basis for most of the fixes you'll find in this book—you'll be referring to them often and learning how and when to use each one.

Before trying any of the following techniques, be sure you know how to tell the difference between a knit and purl stitch (see Figures 20 and 21 on page 15), particularly how it looks just below the needle (see Figure 39 on page 40 and Figure 41 on page 41), and how to find your working yarn (see Figure 2 on page 8).

Unknitting

Unknitting—sometimes called "tinking" ("tink" is "knit" spelled backward)—is like seeing a reverse, slow-motion film of knitting errors as they happen. We all tend to repeat the same mistakes on any project. Unknitting takes us back to the mistake. Undoing the mistake shows what went wrong, giving us the chance to learn.

Here's How to Unknit

Unknitting moves stitches in reverse, undoing each new stitch from the right needle and replacing the old stitch on the left. If you're at the end of a row, leave the full right needle in your right hand, exactly the opposite of what you'd do normally. If you're in the middle of a row, find your working yarn (see page 8) and hold the needle it's attached to in your right hand. The working yarn comes off the back of knit stitches and off the front for purls.

1 The trick to unknitting is to place the left needle tip into the stitch lying right underneath the live stitch next to the tip of your right needle. To do this, pull on the working yarn; the opening created in your stitches points to exactly where to place your left needle.

2 Place your left needle in the opening from front to back (Figures 1 and 2). This captures the stitch from the previous row without twisting it.

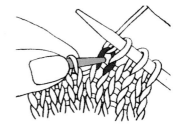

Figure 1: Unknit Step 2

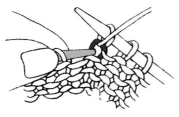

Figure 2: Unpurl Step 2

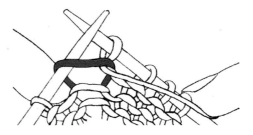

Figure 3: Unpurl Step 3

3 Slip this stitch from right needle to left needle. Pull the working yarn to unravel the stitch. The old stitch now sits on the left needle—one stitch has been unknitted (Figures 3 and 4).

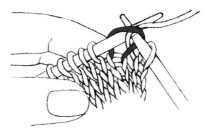

4 Repeat Steps 2 and 3 until you arrive at the mistake.

Figure 4: Unknit Step 4

Vertical Fixes for Stitch Mistakes

While unknitting corrects mistakes horizontally, sometimes it's more efficient to drop down vertically through multiple rows to fix a single dropped or twisted stitch, or even to change a knit stitch into a purl and vice versa.

Dropped Stitch

1 To begin, trace along the column from the dropped stitch up to your needle (Figure 5). Knit or unknit to the stitch to the right of this stitch.

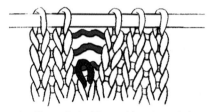

Figure 5: Ladder and hanging stitch

2 To rescue a knit stitch, push the crochet hook through the front of the hanging stitch.

3 Then pick up the first ladder, the one farthest down from the knitting needle. Position the ladder

between tip of the crochet hook and the hanging stitch (Figure 6).

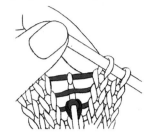

Figure 6: Ladder and stitch on hook

4 Pull the ladder through the stitch, back to front, and drop the rescued stitch off the end of the hook. Continue this maneuver until you've scooped every ladder through the loop below it, then transfer the stitch to the left needle (Figure 7).

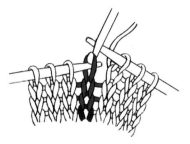

Figure 7: One knit stitch picked up

You've saved one knit stitch. When you pick up a stitch and pull the ladder through with the crochet hook, you mimic vertically what your knitting needles do horizontally when wrapping a stitch.

To rescue a purl stitch, insert the crochet hook from the back of the work to the front to pick up the stitch (Figure 8) and pull the ladder through to the back (Figure 9).

Figure 8: Pick up purl stitch

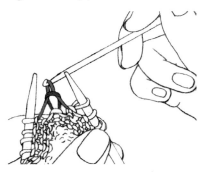

Figure 9: One purl stitch picked up

Sometimes it's easier to fix a purl by turning the work to the knit side, allowing you to pick it up from the front as a knit stitch.

To save a dropped stitch when you're working in garter stitch, alternate between rescuing a knit stitch and a purl stitch from row to row as you hook ladders up to the needle. Remember that, although working garter stitch back and forth means knitting each stitch on each row, what you actually produce is alternating rows of knit stitches (the valleys) and rows of purl stitches (the hills), since the reverse of every knit stitch is a purl stitch.

Any Other Single-Stitch Mistake

Find the vertical stitch column of the mistake and follow it up to the stitches on the needle. Now analyze the stitch pattern. Should the incorrect stitch be a knit or a purl? And what should the stitches be between the mistake and the needle? Knit or unknit to the stitch directly above the mistake. Your working yarn should be in the stitch next to the mistake's column, not right above it. Pull the stitch off the needle at the top of the column containing the stitch to be fixed and unravel it row by row down through the mistake, creating a ladder at each row. Make sure you pick up a knit from the front, resulting in that familiar V stitch shape. Pick up the purl from the back or keep flipping the work so the stitch you're rescuing always appears as a knit stitch when it's facing you.

Unraveling, Then Picking Up Stitches

Unraveling is always my last choice for fixing a mistake, but sometimes it's unavoidable. The trick is to put a brake on so the stitches don't unravel too far and are easy to restore to the needle. Here's how:

1 Find a needle much smaller than the one you've been knitting with to use as your "brake" needle—I use a 24" (60 cm) circular needle, size 1 (2.5 mm). Circular needles have points at both ends, making it simpler to replace captured stitches on the regular needle.

2 Find a row below whatever mess you're removing. With the brake needle, pick up the right leg of every stitch across that row, from one edge to the other (Figure 10). Be careful to stay in the same horizontal row.

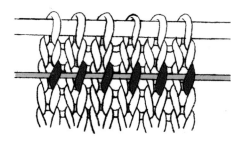

Figure 10: Brake needle in right legs of stitches

3 Take a deep breath. Exhale. Now pull the regular needle out of all your working stitches (Figure 11). Pull the working yarn to unravel.

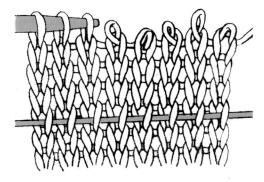

Figure 11: Pull out regular needle

Yep, right down to the brake needle. Go ahead, you can do it.

4 Move all the stitches from the brake needle to your regular needle (Figure 12). Remember to place right stitch legs forward, and make sure the working yarn is coming out of the stitch that will land at the tip of the right needle.

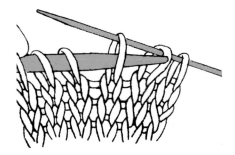

Figure 12: Move stitches to regular needle

chapter 4
Troubleshooting

I tend to look at knitting problems the way my husband looks at The New York Times crossword puzzles: as a collection of intriguing clues. Here you'll find a guide to diagnosing a problem based on its symptoms. This section contains the most frequently encountered problems, diagnoses of what caused the problems, and ways to fix them (and how to avoid them next time). The solutions use one or more of the fixes from Chapter 2 (Fixes You'll Use Again and Again).

Twisted Stitches

PROBLEM: Some of my stitches look like little crossed legs, not Vs. It looks like the Rockettes are dancing across the sweater front.

DIAGNOSIS: Most likely you've twisted some of the stitches. Here's what twisted knit stitches look like (Figure 1):

Figure 1: Twisted knit stitches

It's pretty subtle, unless you happen to be knitting an entire sweater front in, say, shiny red yarn in stockinette stitch, which means all your knit stitches sit up and beg for attention. When stitches are worked through the back leg or front leg randomly, especially in stockinette stitch, the resulting fabric looks like a marching band gone awry.

FIX: If you come to a stitch on the left-hand needle and the stitch's left leg is forward (Figure 2), fix it by inserting your right needle tip into the stitch behind its right leg (Figure 3).

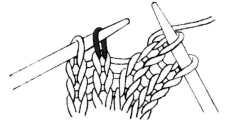

Figure 2: Left leg forward

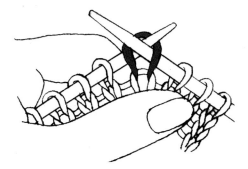

Figure 3: Untwist the stitch

Slip it temporarily onto the right needle, then return the stitch to the left needle with its right leg forward (Figure 4).

Figure 4: Right leg forward

FIX: If you discover that you've twisted a stitch many rows earlier, use the vertical fix to drop down to the twisted stitch, then use your crochet hook to turn it around the right way before picking up the ladders and putting the top stitch back on the needle. (If you have rows of twisted stitches, you may choose to unravel instead of dropping, correcting, and picking up every stitch individually.)

To avoid twisted stitches

When you come to each stitch on the left-hand needle, make sure its right leg is forward before you knit or purl it. A twisted stitch feels tight when you place your needle into it.

Some knitters may twist their stitches because they wrap their yarn around the needle clockwise instead of counterclockwise.

Also, remember that stitches restored to the needle after unraveling or dropping must sit right leg forward. Always. Unless the pattern says to work the stitch through the back leg or loop (abbreviated ktbl or ptbl) for a deliberately twisted effect.

Reversing Directions

PROBLEM: There's a hole in my work a few rows down from the needle, with this weird sideways stitch, and one side of my knitting is longer than the other (Figures 5 and 6).

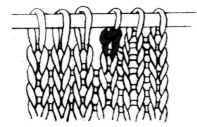

Figure 5: Reversed direction on the needles

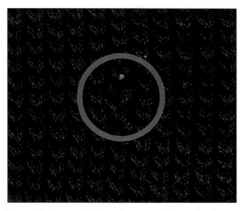

Figure 6: Reversed direction several rows back

DIAGNOSIS: Chances are you reversed direction in the middle of a row after life interrupted your knitting.

✚ **FIX:** The only fix for this is to unknit or unravel to the hole, turn the work around so that the working yarn comes from the first stitch on the right needle, then continue knitting in the correct direction.

To avoid reversing directions

Try to get to the end of the row before you put your knitting down. If that's not possible, remember that *the working yarn is your friend*. It's attached to the last stitch you made, and it should be the stitch closest to the tip of the right-hand needle when you pick up your project again.

Skipped Stitches

PROBLEM: I forgot to knit one of the stitches on my needle—I moved it to the right needle but didn't work it.

DIAGNOSIS: Sometimes you're zipping along in stockinette or garter stitch, right there in Zen knitting, and without noticing, you skip a stitch and knit the next stitch. It looks like this on the needle (Figure 7):

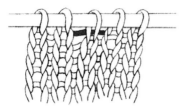

Figure 7: Skipped stitch

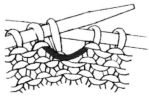 **FIX:** If you catch the skipped stitch within that row, fix by unknitting to the missed stitch, knit it, and go back to Zen knitting.

PROBLEM: The skipped stitch is really noticeable as I work the next row (Figure 8).

Figure 8: Skipped stitch on following row

FIX: Grab the crochet hook and pull what looks like the ladder through a knit stitch from the front or from the back of a purl. The ladder will be lying directly in front or back of the skipped stitch (Figure 9) or in some cases over the stitch and the needle.

Figure 9: Fix skipped stitch on following row

PROBLEM: The skipped stitch is way down there in the fabric (Figure 10).

Figure 10: Skipped stitch down in fabric

FIX: This is a stitch mistake that requires unraveling. It can be hard to see, but a skipped stitch leaves a small gap in the fabric with a missed wrap—and a short ladder—so the vertical fix won't work.

Unravel past the row with the skipped stitch hole and take it from there.

If you notice the hole after the garment is done, repair it from the wrong side with tapestry needle and yarn.

Too Many Stitches

PROBLEM: I have too many stitches on the needle.

DIAGNOSIS: Look for slanted stitches on your needle. If you see any, you may have accidentally made a yarnover (Figures 11 and 12).

Accidental increase by yarnover is easy to do—it happens when you throw the working yarn to the front when making a knit stitch or to the back when making a purl, taking the working yarn over the right needle so that the loop on the needle looks like a stitch. On the knit side, look for one slanted stitch; on the purl side, look for two joined slanting stitches.

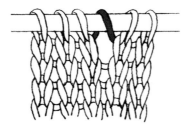

Figure 11: Knit side yarnover—note slant

Figure 12: Purl side yarnover—note slant

⊕ FIX: Unknit to the slanted yarnover—there's your working yarn, on the incorrect side of the work. The yarnover will fall off the needle. Move the working yarn to the back for a knit stitch or to the front for a purl; continue knitting normally.

DIAGNOSIS: If you don't see slanted stitches on the needle, check the knitted fabric for holes. If you find a hole and there's no dropped stitch hanging on, you may have made a yarnover in an earlier row (Figure 13).

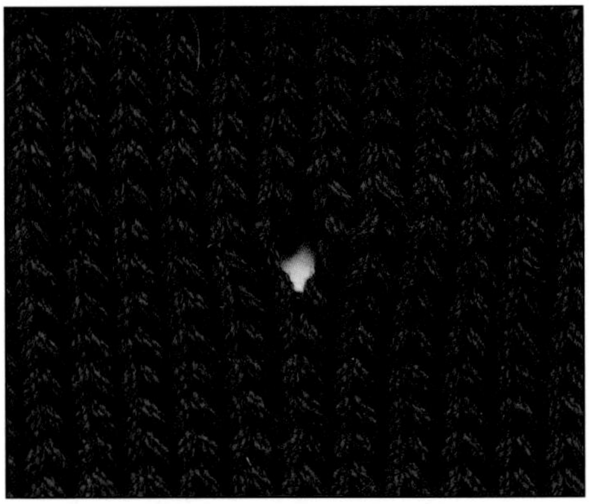

Figure 13: Yarnover on earlier row

To avoid accidental yarnovers

Especially when you're learning to knit or you're working in a pattern that alternates knits and purls, be very careful to move the yarn from front to back between the tips of the needles, not over them.

✚ **FIX:** Unknit or unravel to the hole, move the working yarn to the correct side of the work *between* the needles, and continue knitting.

DIAGNOSIS: You may have knitted the first stitch of the row as if it were two stitches.

This common problem is a variation of the accidental yarnover: the working yarn is thrown over the needle at the end of the row, front to back, instead of under the needle. That pulls the first stitch up so that it looks like two stitches (Figure 14).

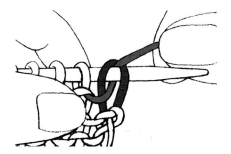

Figure 14: Working yarn thrown over the needle at end of knit row

✚ **FIX:** If you're knitting in stockinette, reverse stockinette, or garter stitch, and you're off by only one stitch, compensate by knitting or purling two stitches together at the beginning or end of a row at that edge. This fix won't work in a stitch pattern such as seed or rib or anything

more complex, especially lace or cable patterns. For patterns like these, it's essential to have the correct number of stitches at all times. Unknit or unravel to the accidental increase and remove it.

DIAGNOSIS: If you're working with yarn that's not tightly plied, you may have split the yarn in a single stitch with the needle point when you placed the needle for the first step of the knit stitch. It's easy to knit the split yarn as two stitches (Figure 15), and the next thing you know, your stitch count is off.

Figure 15: Split stitch

✚ **FIX:** If the split stitch is on the same row you're working, unknit back past that stitch, then knit it again as a single stitch. If the split stitch is farther down in the finished fabric, use the vertical fix to drop down and pick it up as a single stitch.

DIAGNOSIS: You knitted into the bar between the stitches.

Now, about that horizontal strand of yarn between two stitches (Figure 16):

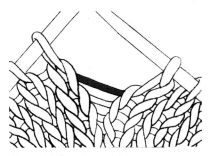

Figure 16: Running stitch

It's called the running stitch, and it's supposed to be there. Sometimes it looks funny, loose, or messy. When in doubt, trace the vertical column of stitches down from each stitch on the needle.

If each stitch on your needle doesn't lead down a continuous vertical column to the cast-on edge, then you know you've accidentally knitted into the running stitch or added a yarnover. Unknit or unravel back to one stitch to the right of the added stitch and take a close look at your work. On the needle, a picked-up running stitch resembles a yarnover. Pull the slanted stitch off the needle. If each stitch on the needle now sits on top of a vertical column, then the problem was a knitted running stitch.

DIAGNOSIS: You forgot one (or more) decreases.

✚ **FIX:** Depends. No, seriously. If you're shaping the armhole of a sweater and you've forgotten to do the last two decreases, but the pattern calls for decreases every other row, then sneak an extra decrease into a decrease-free row. Or, if the decreases are specified on the right side, throw in one (or two) decreases on the wrong side, using the decrease that slants in the correct direction.

If you're working a lace pattern or textured stitch requiring lots of slanted decreases to create the pattern, then it's time to fix. Here, forgotten decreases could throw off the rest of the design. If you've caught the mistake within a few stitches, unknit. If it's rows away, unraveling will ultimately be the easier fix.

Attention, perfectionists

If the armhole will eventually have a sleeve sewn into it or an edging added, then perfect decrease spacing will be lost to the public eye in the seam or edging, especially if decreases are worked at the very beginning or end of rows. If decreases are made one stitch in from the edge, as some patterns require, then only someone looking for them will be able to tell if the spacing is exact. And if someone is staring closely enough at your armhole to notice, well, that's another problem entirely. Think about whether the decreases will show up on the finished garment before you decide which fix you need.

Not Enough Stitches

PROBLEM: I don't have enough stitches on my needle.

DIAGNOSIS: If you count stitches only to discover that there's one too few, look to see if there's a dropped stitch hanging on for dear life. If you find a ladder—this looks exactly like a run in your stocking—you'll find a stitch hanging at its base. That stitch wants nothing more than to climb back and sit comfortably on the needle. If there's a column of stitches that ends before the needle, then, sure enough, you've dropped a stitch (Figure 17).

Figure 17: Dropped stitch

FIX: If at first you don't spot a hanging stitch, look for a hole in the fabric. If you find a stitch just hanging there, go ahead and grab it so it can't drop down farther. Secure the hanger-on with a coil-less safety pin or locking stitch marker. With your crochet hook handy, pick up the stitch as described for vertical fixes (see pages 22–23). If you've worked way past the dropped stitch—I'm talking 6" (15 cm) or more—the vertical fix probably won't work. The ladders will be too short, and the vertically saved stitches may pucker or look uneven. I hate to unravel so much that I usually give the vertical fix a shot, anyway. If the vertical fix fails, you have two choices: to unravel down to the dropped stitch, or if the stitch is near where you'll be seaming or burying yarn ends, leave it for now and secure the stitch later by weaving a yarn tail through it during finishing.

PROBLEM: I dropped several stitches, and if I try to pick one up, the others get worse.

DIAGNOSIS: It's a multi-stitch wreck (Figure 18):

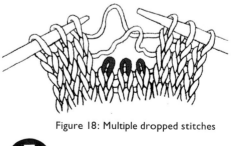

Figure 18: Multiple dropped stitches

FIX: In order to prevent further casualties, first find all those hanging stitches and give them something to grip on to temporarily (Figure 19). My favorite tool for this is a cable needle, but any double-pointed needle works.

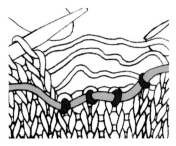

Figure 19: Place dropped stitches on a cable needle

Once the stitches are secured from unraveling any farther, it's a matter of picking up each stitch individually, using the vertical fix technique. Use a crochet hook to pick up the first dropped stitch from the cable needle. Pull each ladder through the stitch (back to front for a knit stitch, front to back for a purl stitch) as you would for a single dropped stitch. Slip the rescued stitch to whichever knitting needle is closer.

Using a crochet hook, walk the next stitch from cable needle to knitting needle. When all the dropped stitches are back on the knitting needle, find your working yarn. If any unworked stitches landed on the right needle, move them onto the left needle, making sure that the right leg of each stitch sits in front of the needle.

Now, holding firmly to both needles with one hand, use your free fingers to tug on the knitted fabric, evening out any slack and returning recovered stitches to shape. Then double-check by following each stitch down vertically to make sure that you didn't accidentally twist a stitch on its way to the needle. If you did, drop the stitch from the needle down to the twisted stitch, straighten it out, and pick it up again with the crochet hook.

PROBLEM: All of the stitches have fallen off the needle (Figure 20).

Figure 20: All stitches off the needle

DIAGNOSIS: This happened to me entirely too often when I first knitted socks. I would blithely pull one double-pointed needle out of the live stitches, thinking the needle I had grabbed was the spare. When off the needle, live stitches tend to bloom like flower petals, twisting around so they don't face the same way.

How do you pick up all those stitches without unraveling farther?

⊕ **FIX:** First, find a needle three or four sizes thinner than the one used for the project. I keep a size 1 (2.5 mm) circular needle in my tool case for this very problem. Hold the skinny needle in your right hand, tip facing left. Working from the right side of the line of loose stitches, gently squeeze the stitches into line between your left thumb and forefinger. Push the needle tip through each stitch one by one. At this point, you're only interested in reseating the stitches, so don't worry if some of the stitches sit with the left leg in front. Once you've got the stitches hanging on to the needle, look closely between each stitch for any stitches you might have missed. Note where they are or secure them with coil-less pins. Now take your original needle and, moving from the left side of the work, slip the recovered stitches onto it one by one. If you come to a dropped stitch, perform the vertical fix. Chances are you'll only have to pull one ladder through any dropped stitch. As you transfer each stitch, make sure its right leg is in front of the needle.

Now that all the stitches are back on the needle, find the working yarn. If it's in the middle of a row, move all the stitches to the left of the working yarn to the left needle and resume your stitch pattern. If it's at the end of the row, begin knitting.

Now, was that worth panicking over?

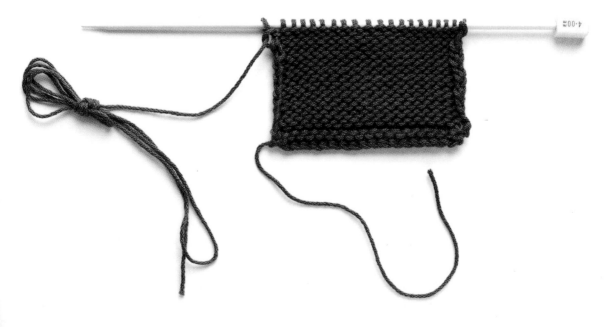

Cables Crossed Incorrectly

PROBLEM: I meant to cross a cable left, but I crossed it right, and that was several rows back (Figure 21).

Figure 21: Cable crossed in the wrong direction

➕ **FIX**: It would be easy to unravel all the rows down past the mistaken cross, but only if you don't mind reworking all those rows. To save time, try a variation on the vertical fix:

1 You'll need a cable needle, crochet hook, stitch holders, and coil-less pins (the big plastic ones are best).

2 Note what row of the pattern you're on, what row the incorrect cross is on, and how many rows sit between the needle and the mistake. Cables tend to cross at regular intervals.

3 Knit or unknit to the cable in question, leaving the working yarn in the last stitch on the right needle to the right of the cable (Figure 22).

Figure 22: Arrive at cable to be fixed

If you're working with slippery or very fine yarn, you might want to put the left needle stitches on a stitch holder, just to make sure they don't get involved.

4 What follows is a vertical fix that mimics how the stitches of a cable are usually made: one stitch group is on a cable needle in front of or behind the work, allowing the other group to be knitted first.

Drop the entire cable from the needle and unravel each cable stitch down through the incorrrect cross (Figure 23).

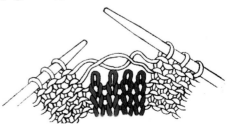

Figure 23: Unravel cable cross

First, isolate the surgical area. Place the stitches that would have been on the cable needle on a single coil-less pin and the other group of cable stitches on a separate pin. Move the "cable needle" pin so that the cable crosses in the correct direction, front or back (Figure 24).

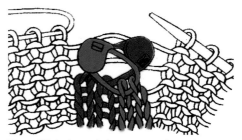

Figure 24: Isolate stitches on two pins and cross in correct direction

5 Now move to the other stitch group. Release the first stitch on the second pin. With the crochet hook, walk that stitch up the ladder to the left needle (Figure 25). Make sure that the stitches aren't twisted and that the ladders are in order. Tug the fabric gently with your free hand to snug the ladders as you go. This column will still look messy and loose.

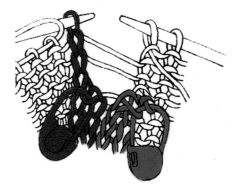

Figure 25: Walk the first stitch up to the needle

6 Take the next stitch in order from the pin and hook it up to the left needle, tightening ladders as you go. Repeat until all stitches not on "cable needle" pin are on the left needle (Figure 26). Knit the restored stitches onto the right needle (Figure 27).

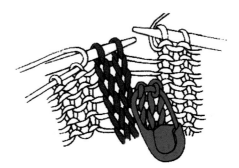

Figure 26: First group of stitches walked to needle

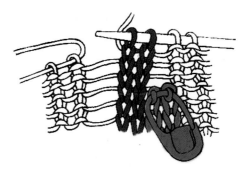

Figure 27: Knit restored stitches onto right needle

7 Place each "cable needle" stitch on a separate pin, leaving the first stitch free (Figure 28).

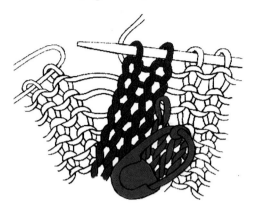

Figure 28: Free the first stitch

8 With the crochet hook, hook the first stitch up through each ladder to the left needle, pulling ladders firmly as you go (Figure 29).

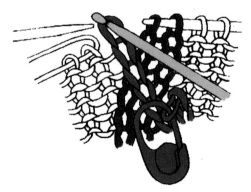

Figure 29: Walk the first stitch to the needle

Repeat Step 8 on the remaining stitches, one by one.

If you moved the left-hand stitches to a holder, replace them on the needle. Locate your working yarn. Work across the corrected cable stitches, then tug them vertically and horizontally until they settle back in place (Figure 30).

Figure 30: Corrected cable

Counting Stitches and Rows

PROBLEM: I lose my place in a stitch pattern because I can't tell when I'm looking at knit or purl or k2tog or yo.

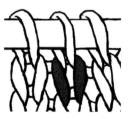 **FIX:** Looking at the last few stitches you've made and the next few to be worked should tell you where you are, and from there you can compare your knitting with the pattern to see where to go next.

Finished stitches tell a story, and sometimes it's handy to be able to read their single letters and short phrases:

A knit stitch looks like a V (Figure 31).

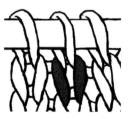

Figure 31: Knit stitches

A purl stitch looks like a slightly curved bump (Figure 32).

Figure 32: Purl stitches

If you look closely at a k2tog (knit two together [Figure 33]) or p2tog (purl two together), you'll see two stitches hanging together off a single stitch above, like twins hanging on to their mother.

Figure 33: K2tog twins

An ssk (slip-slip-knit) decrease looks pretty much the same as a k2tog except that it slants to the left instead of to the right (Figure 34).

Figure 34: Ssk

A yo (yarnover) is easy to spot since it always lies slanted on the needle (Figure 35).

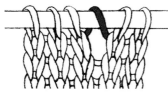

Figure 35: Yarnover slant

When it's farther down into the knitted fabric, the yo creates a hole that looks like this from the knit side (Figure 36).

Figure 36: Hole caused by yarnover (seen from knit side)

And this from the purl side (Figure 37).

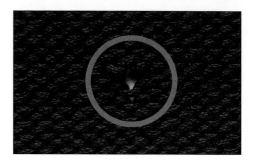

Figure 37: Hole caused by yarnover (seen from purl side)

Now compare the stitches on your needle with the pattern or chart to find which row of the pattern matches the stitches on your needles. Then just pick up where you left off. If your stitches don't match any row of the pattern, you've probably made a mistake and you'll need to unknit a row or two.

PROBLEM: I've lost count of how many rows I've worked.

DIAGNOSIS: Counting the number of rows you've worked can be confusing.
A knit row looks like this (Figure 38).

Figure 38: Knit row

and this right below the needle (Figure 39).

Figure 39: Knit row below needle

A purl row looks like this (Figure 40),

Figure 40: Purl row

and this right below the needle (Figure 41).

Figure 41: Purl row below needle

 **FIX:** Here's how to count rows:

1 Don't count the cast-on row, especially if you used a cable or long-tail cast-on, unless the pattern specifically says to.

2 To count knit rows, find the center of a knit V right above the cast-on row (Figure 42). Follow the column of knit stitches by counting the centers of each knit stitch.

Figure 42: Column of knit stitches

(I count by putting the needle tip into the hole in each knit V, which gives me a tactile point of reference.)

The last row is the one just below the needle—the stitches *on* the needle have yet to be knitted.

3 To count purl rows, look for the purl bumps (Figure 43).

Figure 43: Purl bumps

Notice that the bumps interlock horizontally, like a connected line of smiles and frowns.

When counting purl rows, count either smiles or frowns, not both.

I'm a great believer in using knitting tools to make my projects easier and, well, more fun. I own every kind of row counter and use counters all the time. Yes, I can count rows without them, but why should I? My collection includes coil-less pins, stitch markers for all my lace or Aran work or to mark the center of a vertical line of decreases, stitch holders that open at either end, and a Knit Chek for measuring gauge and checking needle sizes. Some of these tools were bought years ago—they don't wear out, and even the ones that the cats capture for their soccer games (row counters are the most popular) eventually turn up for my use again (I'm the better goalie, thanks to opposable thumbs).

Charts

PROBLEM: All I want to do is make a little baby sweater with a duck on the front, but I can't seem to knit anything that looks like a duck. It's easy to see the duck in the chart (Figure 44), but how does that translate into knitting stitches?

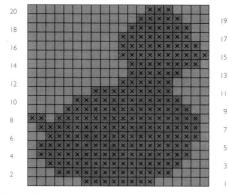

Figure 44: Duck chart

DIAGNOSIS: It's easy for pattern designers to sketch what they want you to do on graph paper, where each square represents one stitch. That's simple enough. But what no one seems to mention about charts is how to read them. That's why most of us face our first chart completely mystified.

If you look closely, you'll see that stitches are a bit wider than they are tall. To make the correct pattern, charts are made up of little rectangles or show the picture somewhat elongated, so your duck may be distorted in the chart. Don't worry; he should come out in the right proportions on your sweater.

FIX: Read charts completely opposite from the way you're reading this page. The first stitch on the chart is in the bottom right-hand (southeast) corner. Read the first row from right to left. If you're working flat—back and forth in rows—read the second row from left to right. Third row from right to left, and so on. Right-side rows are usually read right to left, and wrong-side rows are read left to right (Figure 45).

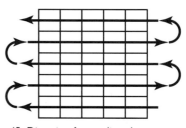

Figure 45: Direction for reading charts

There's a logical reason for this—most of us knit from right to left. When you end a row and flip the right needle full of stitches into your left hand, you knit the next row in the opposite direction. Charts reflect how we knit.

But when you knit in the round, you're knitting on only one side of the fabric. Charts for knitting in the round should be read from right to left for each row. Begin at the bottom of the chart if the project is knitted from bottom to top; at the top of the chart if the project is knitted from the top down.

PROBLEM: Lace charts make my eyes glaze over—I have a hard time following them.

DIAGNOSIS: Each chart is written in a language of symbols or colors, which can be intimidating until you learn the lingo.

FIX: Luckily, most charts offer a key to translate the symbols, just like maps. There are some standard symbols—for example, a blank square usually means "knit on the right side, purl on the wrong side."

Check out the chart for repeats. Many complicated-looking lace patterns can be deconstructed into specific numbers of yarnovers (increases) associated with the same number of decreases. Note the numbers of repeats next to the chart.

It's best to make any chart your own. Some people prefer to write out chart directions, row by row.

Let's analyze this bit of lace chart (Figure 46).

First note the symbols (Figure 47).

These are standard symbols. In fact, the blank or white square representing a knit stitch has such a long history that at one point knit stitches were also known as white stitches. Note also that symbols are listed so you can see the reverse of each stitch: white square for knit, dot in square for purl. The right slash stands for k2tog, the mirror image of ssk, which is represented by a left slash. The dark square means "no stitch" and is a space-holder for a stitch that has been decreased away or for one that will added by increasing later—just ignore it.

Now to the chart:

Note that Rows 1 and 3, the right-side rows, are read right to left, while Rows 2 and 4, the wrong-side rows, are read left to right.

Written out, Row 1's symbols tell you to knit 19 stitches (k19) because you simply skip over the dark "no stitch" squares.

Now look at the pattern of Row 2 closely. The row begins and ends with three knit stitches, because the dot symbol indicates to knit when

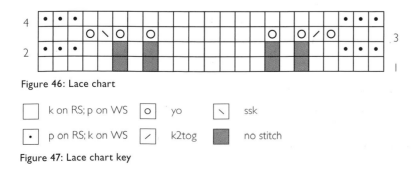

Figure 46: Lace chart

	k on RS; p on WS		o	yo		⟍	ssk
•	p on RS; k on WS		⁄	k2tog			no stitch

Figure 47: Lace chart key

you are on a wrong-side row. The white squares are purled on wrong-side rows. Still skipping over the "no stitch" squares, Row 2 would be written out as k3, p13, k3.

On Row 3, new stitches are added using yarnovers (yo), and the yarnover and decrease symbols are introduced. These yarnovers create new stitches on the needle where the "no stitch" symbols were reserving places for them. The fourth stitch in from each end of the row is a yarnover (yo) increase with a knit two together (k2tog) decrease at the beginning of the row, and a slip-slip-knit (ssk) decrease for the last yarnover in the row. Row 3 would be written out as

k3, yo, k2tog, yo, k1, yo,
k7, yo, k1, yo, ssk, yo, k3.

There are now 23 stitches on the needle. The yarnover/decrease pairs at each end of the pattern cancelled each other out by adding a stitch and immediately decreasing a stitch. The 4 new yarnovers, the ones without companion decreases, added 4 to the stitch count. If you examine the pattern in this row, you will also see that it is symmetrical, with stitches on each side of the center 7 stitches mirroring each other.

Wrong-side Row 4 begins and ends with three knit stitches (k3) like the previous wrong-side row. Written out, Row 4 would read: k3, p17, k3. Notice that each yarnover and decrease of Row 3 is worked as single purl stitch in Row 4.

Try not to let charts overwhelm you. They did me at first, until I grasped that a chart really does represent what a three-dimensional piece of finished knitting will look like—and that I could get my finished knitting to look the same way.

Yarnovers

A yarnover (yo) is a simple added stitch that produces a hole in the knitting, such as the decorative opening that is the basis of most lace patterns. But many directions for a yarnover are so confusing that knitters are stymied. Each yarnover increases the stitch count by one. In a lace or textured pattern, each yarnover is usually paired with a decrease somewhere in the same row to keep the number of stitches constant. To make a yarnover before a knit stitch, just move the working yarn to the front (as if to purl) and knit the next stitch. To make a yarnover before a purl stitch, wrap the working yarn counterclockwise around the right needle once. Following the yarnover and the next stitch, the working yarn will be where it usually is, coming off the back of a knit stitch or the front of a purl stitch.

Color Corrections

First, a couple of definitions of color knitting:

Intarsia is multicolor "picture" knitting using discrete blocks of color (Figure 48).

Fair Isle alternates knitting between two colors at a time (Figure 49).

There are three basic rules for multicolor knitting:

1 Join new colors *without* knotting (see Joining New Yarn Ball, page 56).

2 To prevent holes from forming at color changes, always cross the new color *under* the color you've just knitted with. To cross colors, place your needle in the next stitch and, on the back of the work, cross the new yarn *under* the old yarn (Figure 50).

3 Never carry yarn more than three stitches across the back before crossing it with the color in use. This is called stranding—think of it as catching the carried yarn on the back of the work before it travels over more than three stitches.

Figure 48: Intarsia

Figure 49: Fair Isle

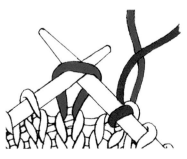

Figure 50: Cross new yarn under old

PROBLEM: My Fair Isle is puckery (Figure 51).

PROBLEM: There are gaps in my Fair Isle knitting where the colors show through from the back side (Figure 51).

Figure 51: Fair Isle with puckers and gaps

DIAGNOSIS: The secret to both intarsia and Fair Isle is in the stranding. Check that the unused colors strand evenly across the back of the work (Figures 52 and 53).

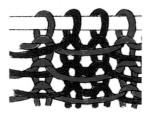

Figure 52: Stranding—cross yarns every few stitches

Figure 53: Back of stranded knitting

The more often you cross the stranded yarns on the back, the less chance you'll have puckering on the front. We tend to pull longer strands tighter. The shorter the strands, the more likely they'll lie flat.

FIX: Make sure to cross the working color *under* the carried color every two or three stitches. Expert color knitters know that they can push this rule, but if you're new to the art, stick with the rule of not carrying the yarn for more than three stitches without crossing. If you break the rule, you may find that the picture on the right side of the garment has some unpleasant puckers where the stranding yarn has pulled in the right-side stitches. Don't go there.

PROBLEM: How do I make stripes without having to cut the yarn every time I change color?

✚ FIX: Strand the unused yarns up the side of the work (Figures 54 and 55).

Use the same stranding rule for carrying different yarns up the side in a stripe pattern as for stranding across the back of the work. Every time you knit to the same side as a resting yarn, pull the working yarn under it, which not only carries the yarn up to the next row but also secures it to the edge of the work so that you don't have to weave in yarn tails during finishing.

Figure 54: Yarn carried up the side of work

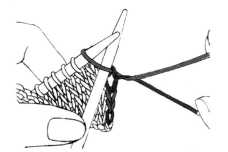

Figure 55: Stranding up side of work

Global strategies for color knitting

Plan ahead a row or two. Years ago, while teaching me to navigate Chicago traffic, a boyfriend insisted, "Always look far down the road. If you see construction in the right lane way ahead, switch to the left lane as soon as you can. Anticipate." The same rule applies to knitting intarsia and Fair Isle. Look ahead in your pattern chart. If in the next row or two you'll need to have a particular color ready to be picked up in a particular place, make sure you carry the color by stranding it across the back to where you'll need it.

You can carry the notion of crossing yarns one step further and bury the yarn tails as you go. If you hate to spend hours during finishing burying yarn ends as much as I do, try this trick. Place the needle in the next stitch and, before wrapping it, lay the yarn tail over the working yarn (Figure 56). Now knit that next stitch. The tail is fastened in. Repeat this until the yarn end is secured. Notice that you're moving the yarn end back and forth across the working yarn.

Make sure, though, that you're not puckering the right side of the work by doing this—it may be necessary to carry the stranded tail more loosely. It's also possible that the yarn you're using simply won't allow this kind of burying, because it's too thin or too inelastic (see Choosing Fibers on page 99). But it's always worth a try. If it doesn't look right, just pull out the buried yarn and weave it in on the back of the work or in the seam allowance.

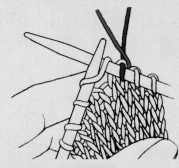

Figure 56: Bury the tail

PROBLEM: I dropped a stitch in my intarsia/Fair Isle.

 **FIX:** Use the vertical fix for stitch mistakes. As you unravel stitches vertically, ignore stranding across the back of the work. And when you walk the stitches back up the ladder, allow the stranding to stay put. Since the stranding will be in a contrasting color in the area you're fixing, it's easy to avoid picking up the wrong color by accident as you hook up the correct color ladders on the way back up to the needle.

PROBLEM: I put in the wrong color. Now my duck has sprouted antlers (Figure 57).

Figure 57: Mistake in color pattern

FIX: This problem can be fixed two ways:

1 Correct the wrong color by unraveling one stitch at a time.

If you've stranded the right color on the reverse of your work but knitted with the wrong color (Figure 58), use the vertical fix.

Drop the stitch from the needle and unravel vertically down through the wrong color stitch (Figure 59).

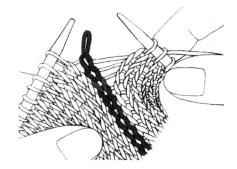

Figure 58: Wrong color used

Figure 59: Begin vertical fix

Then pick up the ladder in the correct color through the stitch on the crochet hook, walking the steps of the ladder back to the needle (Figure 60).

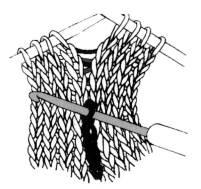

Figure 60: Pick up correct ladder

The incorrect color will now be stranded across the back as it should be.

2 Correct the wrong color using a duplicate stitch.

If the right color isn't behind the wrong color stitch, or if the incorrect color was used in stitches miles down in the fabric, wait until you're finished knitting the piece and cover the mistake with duplicate stitch.

Thread a tapestry needle with the correct color.

Starting from the back of the fabric, push the needle through the bot-

tom point of the knit stitch V (Figure 61). Pull the needle through to the front.

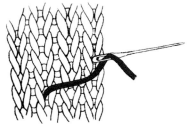

Figure 61: Duplicate stitch Step 1

Insert the needle under both sides of the V of the knit stitch *above* the one to be fixed (Figure 62).

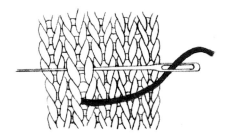

Figure 62: Duplicate stitch Step 2

Pull needle and yarn through. Don't tug. The yarn should cover the right side of the stitch below (Figure 63).

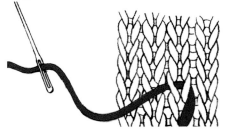

Figure 63: Duplicate stitch Step 3

Insert the needle through the front in the same place you started (Figure 64).

Figure 64: Duplicate stitch complete

The knit stitch is duplicated in the correct color (Figure 65).

Figure 65: Color work corrected with duplicate stitch

You can also use duplicate stitch when an intarsia pattern calls for just an isolated stitch or two of a color, which may be essential to the design but can be tiresome to knit (or may work its way loose during wear).

PROBLEM: I didn't buy enough yarn and can't find any more in the same dye lot. What do I do?

FIX: To blend dye lots, work with one skein for two rows (over and back), cross yarn from the second dye lot under the first at the side, and work over and back with the new yarn. Repeat. However, if you've finished, say, the back and one front of a cardigan in one dye lot, this won't completely solve the problem. Leave the back as is, but unravel the front. Make sure you alternate between dye lot skeins on both fronts and both sleeves. Otherwise, it will be obvious that the colors are different. This also works for hand-dyed yarns.

Some colors, especially whites, are extremely different from dye lot to dye lot. You might prefer to unravel what you've already knitted in one dye lot and start over, mixing both lots from the beginning.

chapter 5
Solving Problems Before They Grow

*W*hen Shirley showed me how to cast on, she was teaching me to solve some knitting problems before they grow. It's a way of looking at problem-solving globally rather than locally. Or heading off annoying and time-consuming problems, like ripping off cast-on edges, before they start.

Casting On

Cable Cast-On

The cast-on Shirley demonstrated was the cable cast-on. It is by far the most useful cast-on. I use it for perhaps 90 percent of my projects. It's easy to do. It gives a neat, finished edge on either side. It can be stretched, which solves a lot of problems when casting on yarns that have no give.

Here's how to do it:

1 Make a slipknot and place it on the left needle (Figures 1–3). This is your first stitch.

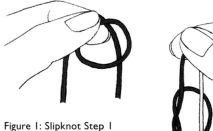

Figure 1: Slipknot Step 1

Figure 2: Slipknot Step 2

Figure 3: First cast-on stitch

2 Knit into the first stitch (Figure 4).

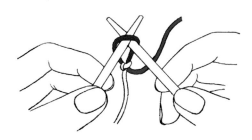

Figure 4: Knit into first stitch

3 Loosen your tension and use the right needle to pull the stitch wide (Figure 5).

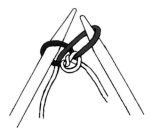

Figure 5: Pull stitch wide

4 With the left needle, pick up the widened stitch from underneath the front leg (Figure 6).

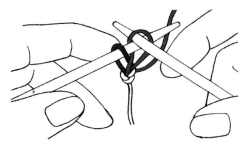

Figure 6: Place loop on left needle

5 Remove the right needle—two stitches have been cast on.

6 With the needle moving as if to knit, insert the right needle *between* the first two stitches on the left needle (Figure 7).

Figure 7: Place needle between two stitches

7 Wrap the yarn around the tip of the right needle as if to knit and bring the new loop forward *between* the first two stitches to make a stitch. Loosen your tension again and use the right needle to pull the new stitch wide. Bring the left needle underneath the front leg to pick up the stitch. Remove the right needle—three stitches have been cast on.

Repeat Steps 6 and 7 until you have cast on the desired number of stitches.

Notice that when you place each new stitch on the needle its left leg may be forward. Odd, but correct. Knit it as it appears.

A few tricks for neat, even stitches

1 Tighten the stitch on the left needle *only* after you've inserted the needle between two stitches to cast on the next stitch. It's easier to get the right needle between the existing stitches when the tension is a little loose. Tightening the yarn after placing the needle also makes sure that needle size determines stitch size.

2 Between Steps 6 and 7, place the pad of your left index finger on top of the last cast-on stitch, then tighten the stitch next to your fingertip (Figure 8).

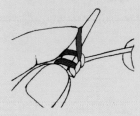

Figure 8: Tighten the stitch

Casting on for ribbing

If you're using smaller-gauge yarn, such as for socks, there's an easy version of the cable cast-on that adds a nice touch. If you want to work in k1, p1 rib, cast on every other stitch by placing the needle in Step 6 as if to purl (Figure 9). This works particularly well for sock cuffs.

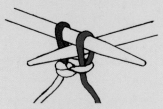

Figure 9: Place needle between two stitches as if to purl

Long-Tail Cast-On

The long-tail cast-on doesn't produce an edge as finished-looking as the cable cast-on, so I tend to avoid it on shawls, scarves, ponchos, or on edges that will show. This cast-on always reminds me of cat's cradle, that string game we use to play as kids.

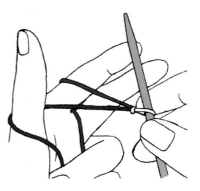

Figure 10: Yarn position for long-tail cast-on

1 Figure out how long the tail should be by wrapping the yarn around the needle once for each stitch you'll be casting on.

2 Make a slipknot and place it on the needle as in Step 1 of the cable cast-on.

3 Drape the long tail to the left of your left thumb and the working yarn (attached to the ball) around to the right of your index finger. Hold the tail and working yarn together between your remaining fingers and your palm. You should be looking at a triangle of yarn (Figure 10).

Figure 11: Dip needle under thumb loop

4 With the needle in your right hand, dip the point under the loop at the front of your thumb (Figure 11).

Then bring the needle tip over the yarn running to the left of your index finger and push it down through the loop around your thumb (Figure 12).

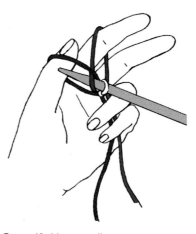

Figure 12: Move needle over running yarn and down through thumb loop

5 Back your thumb out of the loop and use it to tighten the stitch you've just made (Figure 13).

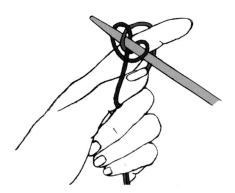

Figure 13: Remove thumb and tighten stitch

6 Tuck your thumb back under the tail to begin the next stitch.

With a little practice, you'll notice that Steps 5 and 6 can be combined into one fluid motion. This insures a consistent tension, with cast-on stitches of equal size.

If your cast-on is too tight, go ahead and cast on using a larger needle, then knit the first row with the correct size needle.

PROBLEM: I just cast on, but now I've knitted less than a row and I'm out of yarn.

DIAGNOSIS: The end of the yarn you've used for your cast-on can dangle there and invite you to pick it up

and knit with it, leaving the working yarn behind.

✚ FIX: Unknit or unravel back to the place where you picked up the tail, then reknit with the working yarn.

> Next time: Tie a bow with the end of the tail; curl it up and secure it with a safety pin; hang something on it—do something to make sure your fingers don't pick it up accidentally. Or cut it to about six inches, long enough to weave in when you're finished.

Backward Loop Cast-On

The simple cast-on, also known as the backward loop cast-on, is the easiest to teach and learn, and the most useless. It looks great on the needle, but as soon as the first stitch is knit, it begins to fall apart. It has very little stability as a cast-on edge. If you use the simple cast-on before joining in the round for a bag or sock, it's nearly impossible to know for sure whether the stitches are twisted.

However, this simple cast-on works for adding stitches in the middle of a row, or a few stitches at the end of a row. Here's how to make it:

1 Hold the needle in your right hand. Loop the working yarn over your left forefinger with the yarn running in front of the loop (Figure 14).

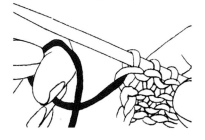

Figure 14: Loop working yarn over finger

2 Place the loop on the needle (Figure 15) and tighten (Figure 16).

Repeat Step 2 until you have cast on as many stitches as you need.

Just don't use it for anything besides adding a few stitches.

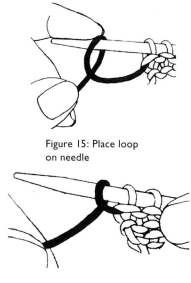

Figure 15: Place loop on needle

Figure 16: Tighten loop

Joining New Yarn

Eventually, you will get to the end of your ball of yarn and need to start a new one. Don't knot. Resist the urge. Tying knots creates all kinds of unnecessary problems. When the knitted garment is worn, yarn knots either poke through to the right side or end up making the wearer feel like the title character in *The Princess and the Pea*. Similarly, if you run across a knot where the manufacturer joined two strands (they're allowed to), you'll want to cut out that knot and treat the remainder of the ball as if it were a new ball.

If you're working back and forth in flat pieces, start a new ball at the side of the work if at all possible. To figure out whether you have enough yarn on the old ball to make it through one more row, measure the remaining length of yarn to see if it is six times the width of the work. If less than six widths remain, do not start the new row, but instead cut a tail about 6" (15 cm) long and save the rest for sewing the garment together.

If you're working in the round, there won't be a side seam. Try to join the new ball at the beginning of the round, which will usually fall at the underarm or back. Again, don't knot.

To join the new ball, place the right needle in the next pattern stitch to knit or purl (following the established pattern). Wrap the new yarn around

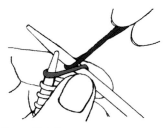

Figure 17: Join new yarn at side of work

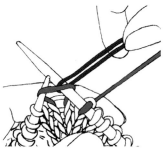

Figure 18: Join new yarn at beginning of round

the needle and continue knitting as usual (Figures 17 and 18).

After you've worked well into the row or round and your stitches seem secure, tighten the tails of the new and old yarns just enough so that the stitches near the join aren't loose and sloppy, but not so much that the fabric puckers.

If you must join new yarn in the middle of your work, be sure to bury the tails as you go (see box on page 47). This weaves in the ends on the reverse side of the work, securing them over a wide area. This reduces the chances of a hole developing later.

Working in the Round

When patterns blithely announce "and join in the round," there's good news and bad news. The good news is that you'll only be knitting on the outside of the fabric. Stockinette stitch? In the round, it's knit every stitch, every row. The bad news is that you must be careful about the join. Because knitting in the round builds concentric stitch circles one on top of another, if the row of cast-on stitches is twisted even once before the join, you'll find yourself knitting a Möbius strip instead of a sock or hat or felted bag or pullover sweater.

When making a project that requires joining in the round, choose the type of cast-on carefully. My preference here is for either the cable or long-tail cast-on (see page 52 and 54). Both produce a defined edge, making it easy to see whether the stitches are lying flat—untwisted—on the needle before joining (Figure 19).

Figure 19: Cable cast-on joined into round

Joining to Work in the Round

PROBLEM: I cast on for a piece that's made in the round, but now it looks like a figure eight (Figure 20).

Figure 20: Möbius cast-on

DIAGNOSIS: One woman I know used the backward loop cast-on for a felted tote bag made of three different fibers knit together. Without knowing it, she'd twisted the base row before joining to knit in the round (Figure 21). She knitted eight inches, assuming that the twist in her knitting would

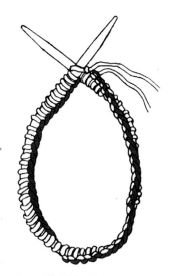

Figure 21: Twisted cast-on

untwist once she took the needles out. Trouble is, a twist in the cast-on permanently twists anything knit in the round.

FIX: In the case of this woman and her bag, she had two choices: rip out and start over, or settle for a bag based on the Möbius strip. I voted for the latter—a Möbius bag could be a work of art—but she was more conservative. And if you're making a sweater, a hat, or any piece that needs to be a tube, the only way to make it right is to unravel it completely and begin with a new cast-on.

PROBLEM: There's a big gap where I joined to work in the round (Figure 22).

Figure 22: Gap at join

DIAGNOSIS: There's a long, loose stitch that leaves a huge gap at the end of the round.

➕ **FIX:** This happens all the time, especially with socks knitted on double-pointed needles from cuff to toe. Try trading the positions of the first and last stitches in the round.

1 Move the first stitch off the left needle onto a spare needle (Figure 23).

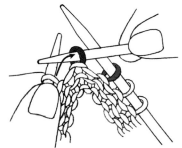

Figure 23: Move first stitch onto a spare needle

2 Move the last stitch from the right needle onto the left (Figure 24).

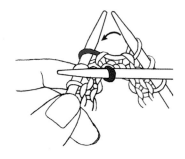

Figure 24: Last stitch from right needle moved onto left needle

3 Finally, place the stitch from the spare needle onto the right needle (Figure 25).

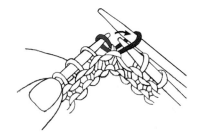

Figure 25: Move stitch from spare needle onto left needle

On the next row, work the stitches in their new order. The gap will have vanished.

Buttonholes

The biggest problem with knitted buttonholes is that they *stretch*. To avoid buttons that unfasten themselves when you're not looking, stick to the simple one-stitch buttonhole (Figure 26): make a yarnover at the point where you want the buttonhole (Figure 27), then on the next row work the yarnover together with the next stitch (Figure 28).

The thicker the yarn, the larger the buttonhole, and vice versa.

Make buttonholes before buying buttons. Buying buttons first just tempts fate. Take your finished piece to the yarn store, lay it out on a table, and try every button that attracts your fancy, pushing it through the buttonhole. Choose a button that seems just a tad big for the hole. When the owner of the cardigan buttons up against the cold, your creation will stay buttoned. Always a good thing.

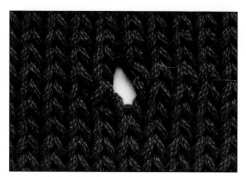

Figure 26: Finished buttonhole

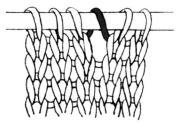

Figure 27: Buttonhole yarnover

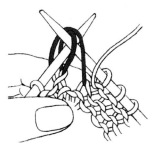

Figure 28: Work buttonhole yarnover with next stitch

Picking Up Stitches

Many patterns will tell you to pick up stitches for collars, sleeves, edgings, and sock gussets. Unfortunately, few of the patterns tell you how or where to pick them up.

"Pick up stitches," "pick up and knit" and "knit up stitches" usually mean the same thing: adding live stitches to an edge where there were none before. Regard directions to pick up and knit the same way you respond to a yellow traffic light: slow down and make your own decision based on what's going on in both directions. Your aim is to pick up and knit an even line of stitches. On a finished sweater or sock or any modular pattern (think mitered squares), if you pick up and knit carefully, the finished product will look like a work of art rather than something made with loving hands at home.

To pick up and knit, you'll only need one knitting needle. Begin at the right edge and work to the left.

1 Place the needle through a stitch at the right edge (Figure 29).

2 Wrap the yarn around the needle as if to knit and pull the loop through the garment (Figure 30). You've made a new stitch that will stay on the needle in your right hand.

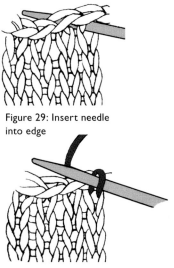

Figure 29: Insert needle into edge

Figure 30: Make the stitch

Repeat Steps 1 and 2 until the correct number of stitches has been picked up and knitted.

However, it's *where* you pick up and knit that's crucial. Every stitch pattern creates a different combination of edge stitches. Rule: Unless the directions tell you otherwise, pick up and knit stitches with the right side of the work facing you.

To pick up and knit on a horizontal edge, where your new stitches will face in the same direction as the old ones, insert the right needle into the middle of a stitch on the row below the bound-off or above the cast-on edge, as illustrated above.

To pick up and knit on a vertical edge, where your new stitches will be perpendicular to the old ones, look carefully at the edge of the fabric. Some patterns specify slipping the first stitch of every row, which makes a smooth edge that looks like a braid (Figure 31). It's very easy to pick up and knit stitches from a slipped-stitch vertical edge. Even if the pattern doesn't say to slip that first stitch, do it. It makes picking up stitches so much easier.

More often, you'll be picking up from an edge that has a series of loops and bumps (Figure 32).

Try to pick up through the loops, between the bumps (Figure 33). It's easier and will give a smoother, more finished look.

Plan ahead. If the pattern *suggests* that you pick up and knit a specific number of stitches over a long distance—say, up one front edge of a cardigan, around the neck, down the opposite edge—count the edge stitches between the bumps. Chances are, the number of picked-up stitches that the pattern specifies is within a few stitches of the number of loops you're actually seeing on your sweater. But to get the exact number of stitches, you may need to pick up and knit inside a

few purl bumps. Or you may need to skip a few edge stitches.

Whatever you do, be consistent in how you pick up and knit stitches. In specifying the number of stitches to pick up, pattern writers are often really telling you to pick up and knit one new stitch for every old stitch on horizontal edges and two stitches for every three rows on vertical or sloped edges, in order to make the neckline or armhole lie flat. For the most part, take the pattern's specified number of picked-up stitches as a suggestion, not instructions written in stone. (For mitered squares or entrelac, numbers of picked-up stitches are non-negotiable. If you change the picked-up numbers, you'll change the size of the module.)

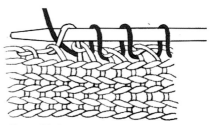

Figure 33: Pick up and knit in loops

PROBLEM: Picking up and knitting the edge stitch leaves an unattractive hole (Figure 34).

Figure 31: Slipped-stitch edge

Figure 32: Knit/purl edge

Figure 34: Gap at edge

FIX: You may need to pick up and knit the stitch in a few different places to find the position that looks right. How can you tell? By doing it. If you pick up several stitches only to find a gap or hole between the pick-up and the edge, pull the right needle back and drop the offending stitches, then reposition the needle and try again.

Try picking up and knitting the stitch farther below the edge. Picking up a stitch inside a bump might tighten up the hole. Rule: Close any holes (Figure 35). If you end up picking up a few more or less stitches than the pattern calls for in order to make the edge smooth and hole-free, that's fine. Just be consistent with the number of stitches picked up—for example, on a cardigan, the picked-up stitches along the neckline from front edge to shoulder seam should be the same on left and right sides. Or if you're picking up stitches around a vest armhole, make sure to take note of the number picked up for the first armhole so that you can pick up an equal number on the second armhole.

Figure 35: Gapless pick-up

PROBLEM: I picked up and knitted the specified number of stitches for the sock gusset, but there's a hole (Figure 36).

FIX: Pick up and knit the number of stitches that the pattern specifies along the edge of the heel flap minus one. Then pick up and knit the slanted stitch in the gap between the flap and the instep stitches (Figure 37).

Figure 36: Pick-up slanted stitch in sock gusset

Figure 37: Sock gusset without hole, after slant pick-up

Errata

PROBLEM: I've checked the pattern over and over and over, and something's just not right. The numbers don't add up, or the piece takes an unexpected turn that isn't shown in the picture.

DIAGNOSIS: In knitting as in life, the first time you try something it probably looks wrong and feels uncomfortable. Do they *really* mean for me to do it this way? Try it—make a leap of faith, follow the directions, and see what you get. The designer may introduce you to a cool new technique. You can always unravel if it's not right.

But sometimes the pattern is just plain wrong. After all, designers and proofreaders are "nearly normal" like the rest of us, and despite their best efforts, a mistake sometimes slips in.

FIX: If you've checked and double-checked both the pattern and the stitches on your needles, and the numbers still don't add up or something looks really wrong, it's time to think about "errata." Errata are the little mistakes that creep into patterns, and depending on where the pattern was published, there are a number of places to look for corrections. In books, they might be on the company's website; in magazines they're often in the next issue as well as on the website; in Web patterns they may be updated online as they are found. If you suspect an error in a pattern, ask around at your local yarn store or knitting group, try a Web search on the pattern name plus errata, or call the publisher directly.

As you become more experienced, you'll learn when to trust your instincts.

Binding Off

Binding off or casting off fastens live stitches off your needles. Luckily, there are only a few variations.

Standard Bind-Off

1 With the right side of the piece facing you, knit the first two stitches. Notice that the working yarn is in the back as usual.

2 Bring the left needle in front of the right and use the point to lift the front leg of the first stitch you knitted (Figure 38).

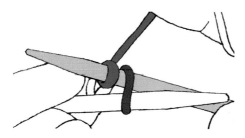

Figure 38: Lift front leg of first stitch

3 Pull the first stitch over the second one and drop it off the end of the needle (Figure 39)—one stitch

Figure 39: One stitch bound off

has been bound off, and one stitch remains on the right needle.

4 Knit a new stitch, so that once again there are two stitches on the right needle.

Repeat Steps 2-4 until one stitch remains. Cut the working yarn, remove the last stitch from the needle, and pass the cut tail through the loop of that last stitch. Pull the end of the cut tail gently while pushing the knot down towards the work (Figure 40).

Figure 40: Push knot down

Purl Bind-Off

If the stitches you need to bind off are purls, you'll follow the same procedure with a couple of minor changes.

1 Purl the first two stitches. Notice your working yarn is in front of the right needle as usual when purling.

2 Bring the left needle behind the right and slip the point of left needle under the *back leg* of the first stitch you purled (Figure 41).

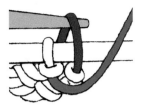

Figure 41: Purl bind-off, Step 2

3 Pull the first stitch over the second and drop it off the end of the right needle—one purl stitch has been bound off, and one stitch remains on the right needle.

4 Purl another stitch.

Repeat Steps 2–4 until one stitch remains, then cut the yarn and secure it as for binding off knit stitches.

PROBLEM: The patterns says "bind off in pattern." What's that mean?

DIAGNOSIS: When the pattern says "bind off in pattern," it means to bind off the knit stitches knitwise and the purl stitches purlwise, as you see them on the needle. To bind off any combination of knits and purls, throw your yarn to the back for a knit stitch and cast off from the front of the needle; throw the yarn to the front for purls and cast off from the back of the needle.

PROBLEM: The bound-off edge is tighter than the previous knit rows.

DIAGNOSIS: The standard bind-off is not elastic and entirely too easy to work tightly, which creates pieces tighter across the bound-off edge than they should be (Figure 42).

Figure 42: Tight bind-off

If you've ever knitted a scarf that seems to come to a point on the bound-off side, you're familiar with the concept.

✚ **FIX:** Bind off using a larger needle or two needles held together in your right hand.

SSK Bind-Off

Lace patterns, or anything worked on needles several sizes bigger than the yarn would normally require, can benefit from this more elastic cast-off. I think of it as the ssk bind-off, because the needle manipulation is exactly the same as used for the slip-slip-knit decrease.

On a right-side row,

1 Knit two stitches.

2 Place the tip of the left needle under the front legs of both stitches from left to right (Figure 43).

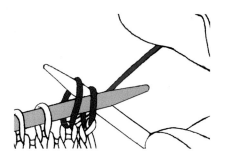

Figure 43: Place needle for ssk bind-off

3 Wrap the yarn around right needle and knit these two stitches together through their back loops—one stitch has been bound off and one remains on the right needle.

4 Knit the next stitch.

Repeat Steps 2–4 until one stitch remains, then cut the yarn and secure it as for the standard bind-off.

SSP Bind-Off

You can get a similar elastic edge on a purl row by purling instead of knitting.

1 Purl two stitches.

2 Bring the left needle in back of the right needle and insert the tip under the back legs of both stitches from left to right (Figure 44).

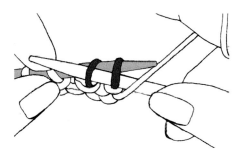

Figure 44: Place needle for ssp bind-off

3 Wrap the yarn and purl these two stitches together—one stitch has been bound off and one remains on the right needle.

4 Purl the next stitch.

Repeat Steps 2–4 until one stitch remains, then cut the yarn and secure it as for the standard bind-off.

Putting It Together

Don't cut corners when it comes to putting your knitted sweater together. Take the time to pin the pieces together and make sure the seams are straight and even. Like pick up and knit, this is a place where careful work pays off.

PROBLEM: The front sides of my sweater are longer than the sides of the back.

DIAGNOSIS: Sometimes, despite your best efforts, you'll find that two pieces aren't the same length—you may have relaxed your tension, producing a looser gauge, simply knitted an extra row or two, or sometimes a stitch pattern hangs longer on, say, the left edge than the right edge (this happened to me recently on a daisy-lace cardigan).

✚ FIX: Match the shorter piece to the longer one by easing in the fabric while pinning the pieces together, then sew.

I find it useful to do this on a flat surface. For straight edges—side and sleeve seams, rectangular bags, pillows—match and pin the bottom corners with right sides together. Next, match and pin the top edges (on garments, usually the base of the armhole). Match and pin at any point on the edges where there's a change from one stitch pattern to another so that ribbing, stripes, or other patterns match at the seam. Pin the midpoint of the seam.

Working first between the center pin and the bottom edge, then between the center pin and top edge, pin the remaining fabric at regular intervals, balancing the extra fabric between the pins—this is called *easing in the fabric*. Continue to add pins halfway between existing pins, which will smooth out the extra fabric, until pins are a few inches apart.

When you're satisfied that the seam will be smooth, thread the yarn you'll use for seaming on a tapestry needle and use a mattress stitch or backstitch to sew the seam. If you choose mattress stitch, it may be necessary to pick up more stitches on the longer piece to match the shorter piece, but if you can match your seam to the way the fabric was pinned, your pieces will match up.

Armholes and Sleeve Caps

You may also need to ease in the fabric to attach the sleeves to your sweater. This can be difficult to visualize because you're joining two curved pieces.

Sew the shoulder seams together. Lay the sweater on a flat surface with the right sides of the front and back facing up so that the shoulder seams lie flat (Figure 45).

Fold the top edge of the sleeve cap in half and mark the midpoint (the center of the sleeve cap) with a pin. Unfold the cap and *with right sides together,* match the pinned center of the sleeve cap to the shoulder seam. The wrong side of the sleeve will be lying centered

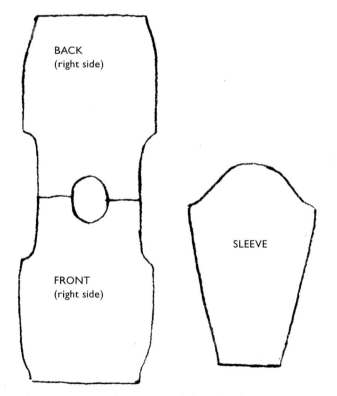

Figure 45: Lay out the sweater with the right sides up

along the shoulder seam (Figure 46). Unfold the sleeve so its right side is facing up and carefully replace the center pin in the same location.

Next, pin the lower edges of the cap to the lower edge of the armholes (Figure 47). Ease in the cap as you add pins at regular intervals until the fabric of the sleeve cap is evenly distributed around the armhole (Figure 48), then sew the pieces together.

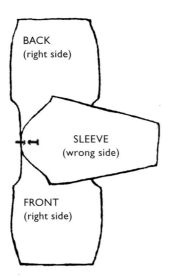

Figure 46: Unfold the sleeve, matching the center to the shoulder seam

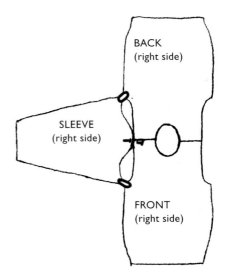

Figure 47: Pin edges of sleeve cap to edges of armhole

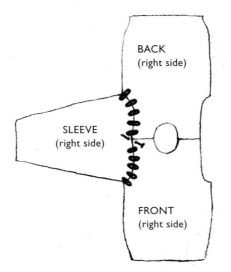

Figure 48: Add pins at regular intervals

Kitchener Stitch, or Grafting

The Kitchener stitch is a great way to finish off the toe of a sock, leaving an invisible join that looks like a row of stitches (Figure 49).

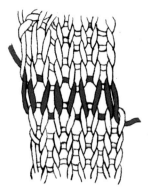

Figure 49: A completed row of Kitchener stitch

To make the Kitchener stitch, divide the stitches to be joined evenly on two needles. Hold the two knitting needles parallel to each other so that the wrong sides of the fabric face each other and so that the yarn tail comes off the right edge. Cut a tail about four times the distance you'll need to graft, then thread the yarn on a tapestry needle (Figure 50). You'll work back and forth between the stitches on the two needles, following a path that mimics a row of knitting.

The key to coming up with an invisible graft is in the first two stitches. Insert the tapestry needle in the first stitch on the front needle *as if to purl,* with the tapestry needle coming through the center of the stitch on top of the knitting needle (Figure 51).

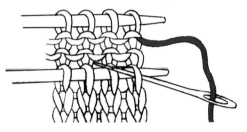

Figure 51: Insert tapestry needle into first front stitch

Pull the needle and yarn through this stitch but leave the stitch on the needle. Next, insert the tapestry needle through the first stitch on the back needle *as if to knit,* with the tapestry needle coming through the center of the stitch from underneath the knitting needle (Figure 52).

Leave the stitch on the needle.

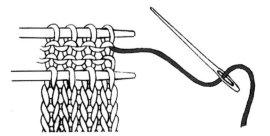

Figure 50: Setup for Kitchener stitch

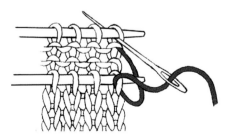

Figure 52: Insert tapestry needle into first back stitch

Now that you're set up, the rest is a breeze:

1 Place the tapestry needle into the first stitch on the front needle as if to knit, pull the yarn through, and slip the stitch off the knitting needle. Insert the tapestry needle into the next stitch on the front knitting needle as if to purl, tighten, and leave the stitch on the knitting needle (Figure 53). Tighten the yarn to match the tension of the original stitches.

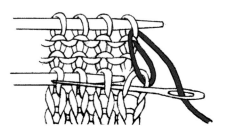

Figure 53: Insert tapestry needle into next front stitch

The secret to invisible weaving is to work *between* the two knitting needles to reach those back-needle stitches.

2 Insert the tapestry needle through the first stitch on the back needle as if to purl (Figure 54), pull the yarn through, tighten, and pull this stitch off needle. As you complete each stitch, pull on the working yarn to adjust the tension of the new grafting stitches to match the size and appearance of the regular stitches.

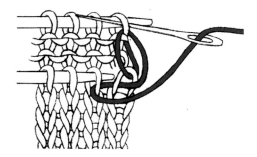

Figure 54: Insert needle into first stitch on back needle

3 Insert the tapestry needle into next stitch on the back needle as if to knit, tighten, and leave the stitch on the needle (Figure 52).

Repeat Steps 1–3 until you've worked all the stitches. To hide the tail, bring it to the wrong side and secure it.

PROBLEM: My Kitchener stitch looks bumpy, as if there are purl stitches across the toe. Isn't the Kitchener stitch supposed to be invisible?

FIX: If your Kitchener stitch shows on the outside, it's time to pull it out. The good news is we usually only Kitchener stitch across a few stitches. Pick out the woven stitches with the point of your tapestry needle to free up the live stitches. With a smaller knitting needle than the one you knitted the sock or hat with, pick up the live stitches. If there are the same number of live stitches as before you tried the Kitchener stitch, great. If not, check for dropped stitches. If you don't see any, then unknit a row or two until the count is correct. Reknit to the point where you need to graft and try again. Remember to move the yarn back and forth between—not over—the knitting needles. It may help to have someone read the directions aloud as you make the join.

Blocking

Admittedly, I'm biased against blocking as a Knit Fix. If sweaters fit—if you measured twice and knitted once—then all you might need is a final light steam press with your iron. Blocking doesn't permanently change the shape of knits. It's a temporary fix, with two exceptions. First, when you knit all your stitches correctly, but end up with uneven stitches. Some yarns will do that. Often a gentle wash will relax the stitches into uniformity. Steam often will do this, too, and I'd try that first.

Second, you must block lace knitting to bring out its glory; unblocked lace looks like a pile of yarn. Pay attention to fiber (see page 99). Dip the lace garment in water, cold if you've knitted with silk or rayon, lukewarm otherwise. Gently squeeze out the excess water; it may be necessary to finish blotting by rolling the lace in a towel. Spread the garment out on a bed, clean rug, or ironing board with a cloth cover—something you can pin to. Pin out the garment, using lots of pins or the long metal pins designed to block lace. (Some lace garments are meant to be blocked but not pinned—read the pattern directions thoroughly.) Lace stretches when wet, so make sure you know your desired finished dimensions and block accordingly. But because lace is more open space than yarn, it dries quickly. (Important to know if you plan on sleeping in the same bed where you block.)

If you must block, keep in mind the three Fs: fiber, flat, and finishing.

Fiber

Wool blocks beautifully, silk and cotton not so beautifully. Yarn memory, give, and weight make a difference. Super fine yarn in any natural fiber tends to block well. If in doubt, review the fiber chart on page 99.

Flat

Particularly if you're blocking pieces before assembling the final garment, make sure that the knitted fabric is smoothed flat. Pins can make ripples in the fabric, especially fabric knitted with finer yarns. Be careful about blocking pieces with dimensions that have to match: side seams should be the same length, hems the same width, etc. Use a measuring tape.

Finishing

Whether you're blocking a sweater or any other assembled garment, remember that this is the last step before wearing. Seams should lie flat, hems straight, shoulders curved. If this reminds you of either sewing or doing your ironing, then you understand blocking.

A final note
Use just a bit of plain, mild soap when washing knits. Most of the special products for washing delicates have some version of fabric softener in them, which tends to weigh down handknits.

chapter 6
Extreme Fixes: Altering When You're Done Knitting

You finish assembling the sweater you've just spent weeks or months knitting. You can't wait to try it on. After all, you've been visualizing this work of art from the time you picked out the pattern and yarn and cast on. In your mind's eye, the sweater fits you the way the one pictured in the pattern fit the model. Maybe better.

Then you look at it in the mirror and feel your stomach lurch. It's so tight you can't breathe, or so big it would fit a member of the Chicago Bears, or the sleeves hang below your hands. Maybe you couldn't even get the thing over your head because the neck is so small.

We have now arrived at Extreme Fixes. We all have to perform them sometime. Here your tool box must expand to include scissors (yes, you might have to cut), lots of long pins (mine are long quilting pins with bright yellow glass heads, fifty to a box), sewing needle and contrast thread, and possibly a sewing machine.

Think of extreme fixing as a series of decisions. First, determine if altering the width or length or neck will solve the problem. If the sweater hangs badly or is wrong in too many ways, then even extreme fixes won't work.

It's not the yarn's fault

Early in my knitting addiction, I made a sweater where the pattern said to begin at one sleeve cuff, knit up the sleeve, cast on for one front and half the back, repeat for second side, finish by stitching back seam. Disaster. It fit like a gorilla suit. The sleeves hung past my hands, the back hung out in a point. Turns out when you knit horizontally instead of vertically, it changes the drape of your finished fabric. I knit the whole sweater and put it together before I discovered this. It irritated me every time I looked at it, but, hey, it wasn't the yarn's fault. And it was beautiful yarn, in eight different colors. I could have fixed the sleeves. The back drape, though, resisted alteration because it was knit horizontally. I took the sweater apart and handed the pieces to my husband. For reasons we prefer not to analyze too deeply, he loves unraveling what I've knitted. A few days later he handed me back a neat pile of wound yarn. Now that yarn is in two of my favorite sweaters, both of which, I am pleased to announce, fit perfectly (see pages 95 and 100).

The Bound-Off Edge

PROBLEM: I knitted a top-down sweater and it's too short or too long at the bound-off edge.

✚ **FIX:** If your sweater was knitted from the top down, shortening or lengthening requires removing the bound-off edge. Relax. This takes no time.

Put the sweater on yourself or whoever is meant to wear it.

To Shorten

1 Try on the sweater and mark the right length with a coil-less pin. Take off the sweater and pin the sleeves up to the right length at the cuff, or if it's the body that is too long, pin it up at the hem. Don the sweater.

Stand back and consider how the sweater looks. If removing inches from the bottom solves the length problem but doesn't throw off the look of the rest of the sweater, then you don't have to take the whole sweater apart. In extreme fixing, you take good news where you find it.

2 Take apart any seams. Find a brake needle (see Unraveling, page 24) and thread it through the row of stitches at the point where you want the new edging to begin. Find the last bind-off stitch, the one where you pulled the cut yarn tail through and tightened. Untie this knot and pull the yarn tail to unravel the bound-off edge.

3 Continue unraveling rows until the brake needle stops the process. Slip stitches from the brake needle to the regular needle, making sure each stitch's right leg sits in front.

4 Knit the new cuff or hem. Bind off loosely in pattern.

To Lengthen

1 Place your brake needle in the last row before the edging.

2 Unravel the bound-off edge as if to shorten.

3 Replace the stitches on the needles (right legs forward) and work until you've added enough length, trying on the sweater frequently. When you've added the number of inches you need, finish with cuff or hemstitch pattern and bind off loosely.

PROBLEM: The neck is wrong—it's too small, and I can't fit my head through my beautiful new sweater. It's knitted from bottom to top, so the neck is the bound-off edge.

✚ **FIX:** Tighten or loosen the neck by removing the bind-off and any finishing.

This is a bit trickier to fix, but you'll find that knitted fabric can be forgiving in this department.

Find a sweater that fits well and has a similar neckline, whether it be crewneck, jewel neck, turtleneck, or what have you. Measure around the neck opening of this sweater—this is your goal measurement. Now measure the sweater to be altered. How much do you want to remove or add?

If it's a matter of opening the neckline just a bit, consider folding the bound-off edge inside and hand-stitching it down (Figure 1).

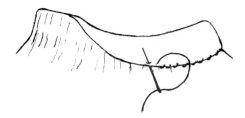

Figure 1: Sew bound-off neckline down on inside

If you need to open the neckline more than a half-inch or so, baste along the new neckline.

Figure 2: Baste along new neckline

Try on the sweater again to recheck your planned neckline. Warning: If this is a raglan-sleeve sweater, make sure that your planned neckline doesn't interfere with the slant of the shoulder shaping. If the neckline looks right, baste a second line about an inch deeper than the first basting (Figure 2), then follow the directions above for removing the bound-off edge and unravel from the bound-off edge to the second line.

Move the recovered stitches onto a circular needle in the same size used for the original neckline (Figure 3). Work the pattern for the neck edge, then bind off loosely.

Figure 3: Move recovered stitches to circular needle

PROBLEM: The neck is too wide, and it looks sloppy and falls off my shoulders.

✚ **FIX:** To tighten the neck, remove the bound-off edge, replace the stitches on the needle, and decrease regularly from picked-up stitches until you reach your goal measurement before working the neck to the desired length. Plan the decreases around the location of shoulder seams, center back and center front, or front opening. Don't bind off too tightly, since you want the neckline to retain elasticity.

I keep trying on the sweater as I knit at this point. My mother is an excellent seamstress and master tailor. Growing up, I watched her repeatedly try things on or stood quite still while she pinned garments on me. There is no substitute for this.

When your new neckline is at the right place, which you'll recognize because it looks good in the mirror and feels right, finish with your chosen edge treatment.

The Cast-On Edge

PROBLEM: The piece is too short or too long at the cast-on edge.

✚ **FIX:** Lengthen or shorten it by removing the cast-on and knitting in the opposite direction.

If you want to shorten or lengthen a sweater that was knitted from the bottom up, take out your scissors and skinny circular needle. It's impossible to unravel from a cast-on edge. You must remove any hemstitch patterns, whether they be ribbing or garter or what have you, because stitches knitted in opposite directions won't line up; they'll be shifted a half-stitch to one side.

1 Decide where you want the new hem/cuff to begin. Measure and mark the same way you would for

> When not to try a clip fix: on modular knits, including entrelac and mitered squares.
>
> Be careful with unraveling any nubby yarn, bouclé, mohair, etc. It can be done but requires teasing the fibers apart with great patience.

bound-off edges (see pages 77 and 78). This is a situation where measuring twice will save your sanity.

Ready? Take a deep breath.

2 Clip one stitch about two rows above the length you've marked. Turn your work around so that you're holding it hem side up.

3 Pull the cut yarn end through the nearest stitch, the one just above it. Before pulling the yarn end through the same stitch again, secure the stitch onto the skinny needle (Figure 4).

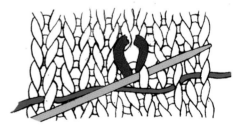

Figure 4: Secure stitch on needle

4 Remove the yarn end from this stitch and repeat across the row or round. If you snipped in the middle of the row, free all the stitches in one direction. Then free the remaining stitches in the opposite direction and secure using the other end of the circular needle. You'll know you're done when you're holding a needle full

of stitches (right legs forward) and the hem comes off in your hand (Figure 5).

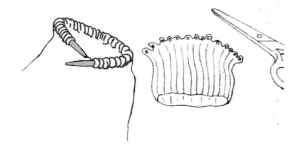

Figure 5: Freed stitches on needle

At this point you may want to close your eyes for a moment and recover. Me, I hear myself shouting, "Yes, it worked."

Move the stitches onto the regular needle, join new yarn, and knit to the correct length. If there is no hemstitch pattern, insert one to disguise the change in direction.

Bind off loosely.

PROBLEM: The cuffs or hems are too tight or too loose.

✚ **FIX:** Use the above fix to remove the cast-on edge and edging pattern.

First, figure out how many stitches narrower or wider the cuff or hem should be. Then decrease or increase

evenly across the first row or two to get to the number of stitches you need, before binding off loosely.

Alternatively, if the cuffs or hem only need to be altered a little, use a needle one or two sizes smaller or larger than the one originally used.

Add Pockets

While we're on the notion of clipping stitches, it's possible to use the technique described above to add a pocket after you're all done knitting.

This is another place where it pays to measure twice. Put on the sweater. Mark where the pocket opening should be (certainly not lower than where your hand can reach comfortably) along with its exact width. While you're at it, mark how long it ought to be, top to bottom (Figure 6).

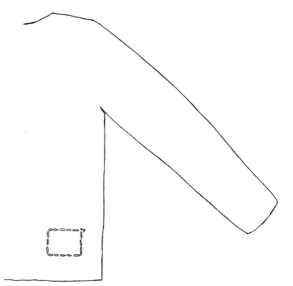

Figure 6: Mark size of pocket

Clip a stitch at the center of the pocket width. Unravel in each direction until the opening is the right size, securing both upper and lower freed stitches onto separate needles (Figure 7). (Skinny double-point needles would be best to pick up the stitches here.)

For the pocket lining, knit the stitches downward from the upper opening in stockinette stitch. The knit side of the pocket faces the inside of sweater front. Increase one stitch at the beginning of each row for an inch or two, depending on the size of your pocket. Then knit plain until about an inch above where you'd like the pocket to end (knitting stretches) and bind off.

For the lower edge opening, knit upward in a contrasting stitch pattern for about an inch. Bind off (Figure 8).

On the inside, sew the sides and bottom of the pocket, making sure that sewing stitches don't show through on the front of your sweater.

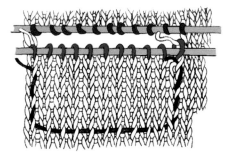

Figure 7: Place pocket stitches on needles

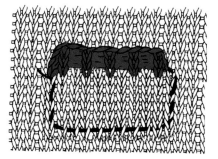

Figure 8: Knit pocket edge

Altering at Seams

PROBLEM: The body and/or sleeves of my sweater are too narrow.

 **FIX:** To add width, measure how much wider the body of the sweater needs to be. Measure from hem to underarm. Does the sweater fit at the underarm? Do the sleeves fit in the area of your biceps? My preference is always to add width at body and sleeves, together. If the underarm/sleeve can be widened by the same amount as the side seam, it's a slightly easier fix—you can knit the panels so that they run from the sweater hem through the underarm and down to the cuff, making the altered sweater hang better. You'll knit two panels—gussets—to your measurements.

1 Take apart the side, underarm, and sleeve seams. Measure the body from the hem to the underarm and the sleeve from the underarm to the cuff. Add these numbers for the total length of each gusset. Decide how much width you'll need to add.

2 Cut two pieces of muslin or other fabric to the length and width you decided on in Step 1. Pin the pieces into the side and sleeve seams and try on the sweater (Figure 9). Does it fit better? Does it need to be wider or narrower? Does it change the drape of the rest of the garment? Make

Figure 9: Pin in muslin gusset

adjustments until you're satisfied that the altered sweater will fit properly.

3 Cast on the width of your muslin on each side, adding one extra stitch at each edge for a seam allowance.

4 Decide whether to knit the panel in the same pattern as the rest of the sweater or in a complementary

pattern. Work the panel to the length you measured in Step 1.

5 Pin the gussets to the front and back of the sweater and into the sleeves. Try on the sweater to check for fit.

6 Sew in the gussets.

If the sleeves fit fine, you may want to shape this panel and insert it in the body only. Decrease regularly to taper the panel to a point, which will fit right at the junction of sleeve seam and under-arm (Figure 10).

Just keep in mind that there's going to be a meeting of the gusset's point,

sleeve, front, and back right at the underarm. That's a lot going on in tiny space, and increases the chance of accidentally altering the drape of the sweater. If you run the gussets from sweater hem to sleeve hem, it opens up the underarm and spreads the assembly stitching over a wider space.

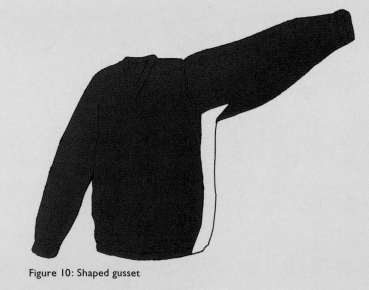

Figure 10: Shaped gusset

Subtracting Body or Sleeve Width

PROBLEM: I made the sweater way too large; it would fit a linebacker better than it fits me.

✚ **FIX:** It is possible to make a sweater smaller, but it requires a sewing machine.

1 Put on the sweater, then pin the sides or sleeves to the correct width.

2 Turn the sweater inside-out. Take out a needle and thread and baste along the marked pin line on each piece (Figure 11). Remove the pins and take out the seams under the arms at the sides and sleeves. Try on the sweater again for fit. It's easy to change the basting if the piece doesn't fit now.

3 Set the stitch length on the sewing machine to make sure your stitches don't pucker the knitted fabric. Stitch a line parallel to your basting on each piece one-half inch from where the new seam will fall, between the basting and the edge of the piece. Now stitch it again, right on top of the first line (Figure 12).

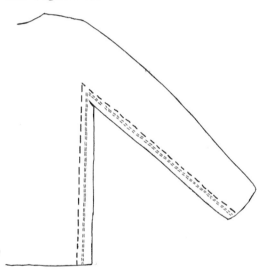

Figure 12: Machine-stitch a double line

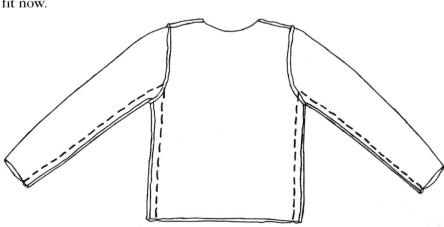

Figure 11: Pin and baste to fit

4 Pin the fronts and backs together with the right sides facing each other. Machine-stitch the new seams along your basted line (Figure 13).

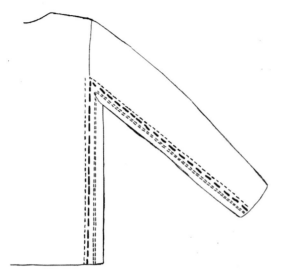

Figure 13: Machine-stitch new seam

Press seams open.

Try on the sweater to double-check the new fit. Be certain this is it, because the next step involves cutting away the excess seam allowance.

5 Ready? See the lines of stitching you've made? There should be seam stitches and that second line of double stitches parallel to the seam, closer to the edge of the knitted piece (Figure 14).

Trim the seam allowance edge just outside the double-stitching, being care-ful not to cut your machine stitching (Figure 15). This double-stitching will stop your sweater from unraveling all the way to the new seam.

If you'd like to avoid this particu-lar extreme fix next time, see Chapter 7: Test-Driving.

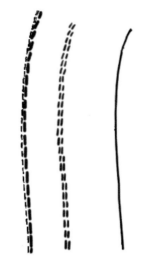

Figure 14: Sweater ready to cut

Figure 15: Trim excess fabric

chapter 7
Test-Driving

*T*oo often we just want to start knitting and forget the preliminaries. I certainly want to. When Shirley helped me take out the cast-on edge of my first sweater, it seemed to take forever. I hoped never to have to do it again.

But of course I would do it again unless I figured out what to do differently next time. As it happened, I needed to learn that dreaming up a sweater should be immediately followed by taking the idea for a test-drive before beginning to knit the project.

It may not be a coincidence that at this point in my knitting career, my real job often took me out to test-drive cars. I'd ask engineers from different auto companies how they came up with new cars. They said that they tested every part constantly, and if something didn't work the way they wanted it to, they figured out why. Did they get frustrated? No, they enjoyed the process. They learned from and capitalized on their mistakes.

My father-in-law would have loved these guys.

It turns out it's a lot of fun to dream up a knitting project (pattern, fiber), plan it out on paper (gauge, fit, pattern changes), then figure out if it's doable in real life (actually knitting the gauge swatch). What follows are the lessons I learned from my own knitting test track.

Gauge

Gauge is the combination of four variables: yarn, knitting needle size, stitch pattern, and your style of knitting tension (loose, tight, average). The designer of a pattern wants you to know that if you'd like to reproduce the sweater in the photo, you'll need to come up with a combination of these four variables that produces the same number of stitches per inch (or, more commonly, four inches). This is called the "gauge" or, in European patterns, "tension." What may have attracted you to the sweater was the picture, but before picking out yarn to make your own version you'll need to figure out how to match the designer's gauge.

Gauge is directly related to the circumference of the yarn. The heavier and thicker the yarn, the fewer stitches

you'll knit per inch. For example, the really fat yarn that knits up instantly on size 15 to 35 needles probably makes no more than two stitches per inch. Think about that: each stitch is one-half inch wide, wider than shoelaces. It will look bulky knitted up in a sweater or scarf or hat. Conversely, the thinner the yarn, the more stitches you'll make per inch. Many sock-weight yarns knit up on size 1 (2.5 mm) needles at seven stitches per inch.

So, how can you tell if a yarn is two stitches per inch or three or five? If the yarn is American-made, the ball band will read something like "4½ sts/inch on #8 needles," or "18 sts and 30 rows/4 inches (10 cm) on #8 needles." Translation: The yarn company recommends that this yarn be knit on U.S. size 8 needles and that, in stockinette stitch, this produces an average of four and a half stitches per horizontal inch and seven and a half rows per vertical inch. If the yarn is made outside the United States, the same information will probably be indicated in icons. Look for a square that resembles a dab of graph paper labeled "10 cm," with one number under the icon and another number next to it. The number under the icon usually gives the recommended number of stitches or rows per 10 cm (which equals, conveniently, 4"). Near the graph paper icon will be an icon that looks like crossed knitting needles, with numbers attached, like "4½–5," which denotes metric sizes, and sometimes the corresponding U.S. needle sizes, like "U.S. 7-8."

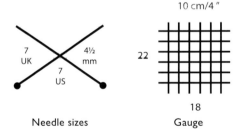

Needle sizes   Gauge

Usually we knit 4" × 4" (10 cm × 10 cm) samples called *gauge swatches.* Cast on the number of stitches and work the number of rows that the pattern says will produce 4" (10 cm). If the pattern gives gauge in stockinette stitch but the garment itself is knit in another stitch pattern, go ahead and make the stockinette gauge. But make sure you make another sample swatch in the stitch pattern. You want to know what your yarn is going to look like in the stitch pattern, you want to practice the stitches with this particular yarn, and you want to be able to measure the number of stitches per inch in the stitch pattern.

For example, if your pattern includes cables, knit a swatch wide enough to contain at least one cable and long enough to cross the cable once or twice. Cables tend to pull in the width of a knitted piece, and you want to know how large this combination of yarn, needles, and pattern stitch will be.

Measure the swatch. Note the length and width of the swatch, then wash it the way you plan to wash the finished garment. When the swatch is dry, measure it again. If it has shrunk, rethink either how to wash the garment or allow for shrinkage in the size of the garment you make.

Got Gauge?

1 If the stockinette or pattern stitch section of your gauge swatch measures four inches, hey, wonderful, you got gauge on the first try.

2 If the stockinette or pattern stitch measures less than four inches, try the swatch again using larger needles.

3 If the stockinette or pattern stitch measures more than four inches, make the swatch again using smaller needles.

Don't try to vary your tension. Tension is your constant variable: you knit the way you knit. Your tension is different from mine.

To see if the way you've been knitting will make the right size sweater, check how many stitches the pattern details for your size across the back. Divide the number of back stitches by the number of stitches in your swatch. Then multiply that number by the width of your swatch. The number you come up with will be half the circumference of your sweater.

For example, if the sample swatch was made over 20 stitches and is 5" wide, and the pattern specifies 100 stitches across the back above the bottom ribbing, divide the 100 stitches (across the back) by 20 stitches (across the swatch). The back will be 5 times the width of the swatch, which is 5" across. The back will be 25" across, and the finished sweater will be about 50" around.

Is this what you're shooting for? If not, make another gauge swatch. If a sweater that's 42" around will fit you better, it'll save you a lot of time and agony to get the gauge right before you cast on for the sweater itself.

Sometimes a particular yarn just isn't right for a particular pattern. One woman came to me for help with a vest she was knitting out of heavy-worsted yarn on size 2 (2.75 or 3 mm) needles.

How far can you push gauge?

You can't always get the same gauge the pattern calls for with a particular combination of yarn, needles, stitch pattern, and your tension. If the swatch measures too big even after changing needle sizes, consider using the pattern's stitch numbers for a smaller garment size, but make sure the number of stitches cast on for the back divided by your stitches per inch is the width you want at the hem.

On the other hand, if the swatch measures too small, consider using the pattern's numbers for a larger size, checking the math as noted above.

Why was she knitting a yarn that is happier on size 8 needles on size 2? Because, she said, that was the only way she could get the gauge called for by the printed pattern. The pattern was designed to be knitted with superfine yarn (see Yarn Weights chart, page 92). When medium-weight yarn is knitted on needles meant for superfine yarn, it produces a hard fabric. This vest felt like chain mail. She needed to pick a new pattern or a new yarn.

Swatching for gauge is test-driving your yarn. If you like the way your yarn looks in the sample swatch, you'll probably like it in the finished garment.

Don't let the arithmetic of gauge scare you away from thinking about it. It is just arithmetic—when did we learn multiplication and division, second grade? And nowadays there are these wonderful little calculators. Joking aside, it's a lot easier on the nervous system to knit a gauge swatch and pull out your calculator for a test-drive than it is to take scissors to a finished sweater.

Yarn Weights

New Standard Yarn Numbers and Names

1 SUPERFINE	2 FINE	3 LIGHT	4 MEDIUM	5 BULKY	6 SUPER BULKY
TRADITIONAL NAMES					
Sock Fingering Baby Jumper Lace	Sport Baby	DK Light Worsted	Worsted Afghan Aran	Chunky Craft Rug	Bulky Roving
STOCKINETTE STITCH GAUGE RANGE (in stitches per 4"/10 cm)					
27–32	23–26	21–24	16–20	12–15	6–11
RECOMMENDED METRIC NEEDLE (in millimeters–mm)					
2.25–3.25	3.25–3.75	3.75–4.5	4.5–5.5	5.5–8	8 and up
RECOMMENDED U.S. NEEDLE					
1–3	3–5	5–7	7–9	9–11	11 and up

Fit

Secretly, I love my handknit sweaters because they fit. The length is just right, hiding my figure ickies and accentuating the positive. Same with the width. The sleeves are the right length, not too long, not too short. And have you ever worn a pair of handknitted socks, where the foot is tailored to yours? Heaven. How is this magic wrought? By knowing how to take measurements and understanding the concept of ease.

First of all, forget the notion of sweater or sock "size." Patterns differ as to what they regard as small, medium, or large. When looking at a pattern, don't think, "Well, I usually wear a medium," knit the middle size sweater, and expect it to fit. So here's a new cliché: measure twice, knit once. First measure whoever will wear the knitted piece. And you will always measure gauge (see Gauge, page 88).

Ease

"Ease" means comfort. In clothes, ease refers to the extra inches added to garments for them to hang comfortably around the body. If you've got a 36" bust and 36" hips and want to have a sweater fit the way Marilyn Monroe's dress fit for President John F. Kennedy's 1962 birthday bash at Madison Square Garden (hint: legend has it that she had to be sewn into it), then by all means knit a sweater that measures 34"-36" around the fullest part of the chest. If you're like me and like to breathe, then add about 4" to your chest measurement—that's the "ease"—and knit a sweater that's 40" around. Or if you like a tighter sweater, go for 2" ease. (Some patterns will give you an indication of how much ease they're assuming you'll want; some even go so far as to tell you right out that they've designed the 36" sweater to fit the 33" person.) Simple but crucial.

Revising a Pattern

If you think of "revising" as "re-seeing," then I have a terrible habit of revising patterns. I don't want to design my own patterns. But I adore changing a lace shawl pattern into a pullover or changing a short-sleeve T-shirt into a long-sleeved jacket. Better yet, I love having something that fits perfectly—if I'm making other changes, it's no more trouble to alter the pattern for a custom fit at the same time. After all, who is going to wear this garment? Me and mine or the pattern designer?

There are a few basics you need to know before revising a pattern. Let's use the example of a sweater pattern.

Sweaters are Basically Squares

Since knitted stitches are nearly square, the joyous thing about knitted garments is that all are some variation on a theme of squares. Even rounded edges such as armholes are squares with smaller squares taken out.

To find the best dimensions for a garment, fish a sweater out of the closet that fits you particularly well. Spread it out, front down, on a flat surface. (My house has mostly cluttered surfaces, so this tends to take place on the bed.) Pull out a tape measure to fill in the blanks on the drawing at left.

A = width of back hem. This number can remain your secret, so be honest about it. Notice that the measurement of the hem is bigger than the measurement of your hips. The extra inches in the hem are referred to as "ease" (see Fit on page 93).

B = length from underarm seam to hem.

C = back neck length, measured from collar seam to hem.

D = sleeve length, from cap seam to sleeve cuff.

With this information in hand, you can make a number of changes with only minimum arithmetic.

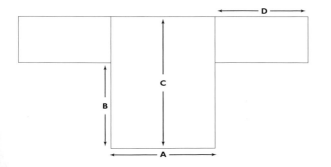

Widen or Lengthen Using Gauge

One of the easiest ways to alter a pattern is to get your gauge to do it for you (see Gauge on page 88). One of my favorite sweaters comes from a Leigh Radford pattern (*Interweave Knits*, Spring 2002) for a kimono-shaped sweater that had a 52" finished chest. Too wide for little me. But all the Kandinsky-inspired intarsia shapes pictured on four pages of multicolor charts were too enticing to pass up just because of a minor problem of size. The pattern specified a gauge of 4.25 stitches per inch, which translates to a heavy worsted-weight, and casting on 110 stitches for the back.

Simple arithmetic: 110 stitches divided by 4.25 stitches per inch comes to just under 26". The back was half the circumference of the sweater, so twice 26" equals 52". I didn't want to change those gorgeous charts, so the number of stitches to cast on had to stay at 110. I found thinner yarn that knitted at 5 stitches per inch: 110 divided by 5 stitches per inch shrunk the back width to 22", or a circumference of 44". Perfect. Of course, using thinner yarn also meant the length and sleeves would be shorter, but that worked, too, since I'm 5'2" tall on a good day.

Gauge widens and lengthens simultaneously, or, as in my example, narrows and shortens.

Kandinsky sweater

Lengthen or Shorten with the Number of Rows

By changing the number of rows you knit, you can cut or add to the length of a sweater or sleeve in any stitch pattern that's not wildly complex. Look at your knitted gauge and count the rows per inch (see Gauge on page 88). If the sweater pattern is too short or long, add or subtract rows before you begin the underarm decreases. If the stitch pattern is complicated, simply look for the pattern repeat. If you want to alter a fisherman sweater with cables and bobbles, see if at some point in the chart the pattern starts all over again. Measure the number of rows in the repeat—that's what can easily be added or subtracted before underarm decreases. In my Kandinsky intarsia example, which never repeated a knitted motif, I could have lengthened the sweater by adding rows of background color before starting the charts, which would have added inches at the lower edge. It's also possible to cut the length of intarsia patterns by cutting off part of the picture. (Remember the world map pullover pattern from *Vogue Knitting* in 1991? One of my sleeves lost New Zealand in the shortening process.)

Narrow or Widen with the Number of Stitches

This can be as easy as altering with gauge. All you need to know is the number of stitches per inch (see Gauge, page 88) you're getting from your particular combination of yarn and needles. This is the gauge you actually produced in your sample swatch. To simplify things, let's say that your gauge and the gauge specified in your pattern are the same, five stitches per inch, and you want to add 4" to a cardigan sweater's width. To widen by 4", multiply by 5 stitches per inch to discover that 20 stitches need to be added. Half the garment's width is cast on in the back, so you'll cast on 10 extra stitches on the back. The right and left front pieces are each one-fourth of the garment's circumference, so you'll cast on an additional 5 stitches to each.

Narrowing or widening the pattern is a simple matter if your design involves stockinette, garter, seed stitch, or any motif that repeats in a few stitches. On complicated patterns such as lace or cables, it's harder but not impossible to alter width as you would for length.

You'll also need to figure out what to do with the extra stitches when you get to the armhole, neck, or shoulder shaping. Don't alter the number of stitches to bind off at the armhole, as fitting the sleeve cap into the armhole is tricky enough. If you need to bind off the extra stitches in the neck area, do it gradually. See if you can sneak them into the shoulders; unless the sweater is very fitted through the shoulders, you may be able to leave the extra stitches in the shoulders, and bind them off as you finish each piece.

DKNY Enchanted Forest Sweater

In 1992, a few years after knitting took hold of me, the now-classic Enchanted Forest sweater pattern designed by Donna Karan appeared in *Vogue Knitting*. In it, cables, bobbles, seed stitch, moss stitch, and slipped stitches created a monochrome picture of a forest, complete with the moon overhead. Could I do it? I had no idea, but I had to try.

However, if I actually wanted to wear it, the sweater would need to be sized down from 58¼" around and 26¼" long. Otherwise, it would be a long flag on a short stick, as we would have said where I grew up in Kansas. The pattern called for thick yarn doubled and knit tightly. My local yarn store came up with oyster white DK-weight wool, but even reducing yarn gauge didn't cut the width down enough. It was time to deforest.

Logically, to narrow a sweater, it's necessary to cut each front panel of a cardigan by the same number of stitches, and the back by twice that amount. I analyzed the stitch charts for pattern repeats. But none of Karan's trees was alike. I looked and looked at the charts. My "aha!" moment came when I noticed that an evergreen on the right front was the same width (though not height) as one on the left front. Since the back chart width was a combination of the two front charts, I could delete four trees in width: one from each front, two from the back. Doing this meant I had to move the armholes on the charts, which I did without changing the stitch counts. Armholes and sleeve caps have to fit together like puzzle pieces, and I didn't want to mess with those.

The sweater fits. I still wear it. No one but Donna Karan would notice the missing trees.

Deforested Enchanted Forest

Choosing Fibers

So, you're enjoying one of those moments of knitter nirvana, standing in the yarn store, ready to take on your next project, surrounded by color and texture and choices. It's right here that you want to know how a particular yarn will act. That depends on what the yarn is made of.

Yarn Behavior

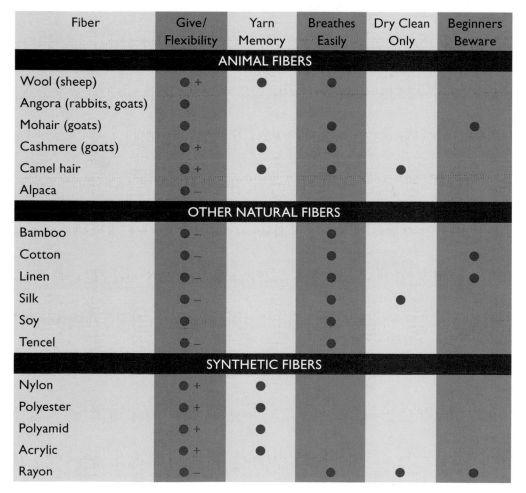

Fiber	Give/ Flexibility	Yarn Memory	Breathes Easily	Dry Clean Only	Beginners Beware
ANIMAL FIBERS					
Wool (sheep)	● +	●	●		
Angora (rabbits, goats)	●				
Mohair (goats)	●		●		●
Cashmere (goats)	● +	●	●		
Camel hair	● +	●	●	●	
Alpaca	● −				
OTHER NATURAL FIBERS					
Bamboo	● −		●		
Cotton	● −		●		●
Linen	● −		●		●
Silk	● −		●	●	
Soy	●		●		
Tencel	● −		●		
SYNTHETIC FIBERS					
Nylon	● +	●			
Polyester	● +	●			
Polyamid	● +	●			
Acrylic	● +	●			
Rayon	● −		●	●	●

ANIMAL FIBERS include wool from sheep, such as Merino and Shetland wool; angora from rabbits or goats; mohair and cashmere, also from goats; camel hair; and alpaca, from the animal of the same name.

All of these except alpaca tend to be flexible—pull on the fiber and it will have a bit of elasticity in it. This means it's easy to knit with and stitches will spring into a uniform size. Wool, camel hair, and cashmere are the most flexible; angora and mohair are less so. Alpaca, though wonderfully soft and light, has no give, and the finished product will stretch in length. It's warm, soft, and fuzzy, but otherwise unlike wool.

Translated into finished knitting fabric, the more flexible the fiber, the more likely it is to drape well. Garments knitted out of these will hold their shape. Fabric with great flexibility seems to float, no matter how thick it is.

On the other hand, the complicated fisherman-style sweater I made for my husband early in my knitting career out of worsted-weight alpaca seemed to grow a foot in length the first time he wore it, as if gravity affected it more than the wool sweater I'd also made him. It was an expensive lesson in how fiber can act.

NATURAL NON-ANIMAL FIBERS—cotton, silk, linen, rayon, Tencel, soy, bamboo—tend to have no elasticity at all unless the yarn is

Cotton stretches, making the sleeves grow from three-quarter to full length

spun with wool or a synthetic such as acrylic or nylon. Pure cotton, silk, or linen knitted garments hang straight and lank, with a fluid drape. These fibers perform well in warm weather, but garments knit from them will tend to stretch and won't snap back to their original size.

My two favorite sweaters are knitted from cotton yarn. The Kandinsky sweater (see Widen or Lengthen Using Gauge, page 95) is made with cotton yarn spun with 1 percent Lycra, just enough to make it slightly elastic. That sweater has held its shape and length for several years now. The other favorite is a sweater of mitered squares combining perhaps twenty different yarns, most of them cotton. By the time I made it, I'd learned to allow room for cotton to grow. That's why the sleeves, originally knitted three-quarter length, now reach the wrist, where I want them to be.

SYNTHETIC FIBERS—nylon, polyester, polyamide, acrylic—can offer a fair amount of give. If the yarn label says "microfiber," that means it contains ultrafine synthetic fibers, most commonly polyester. Microfiber behaves like polyester or acrylic, but feels soft and silky. Acrylic usually can be washed and dried. Good quality acrylic yarns feel and drape just like wool; cheaper acrylics feel a bit like a plastic bag.

Back to your moment of yarn store nirvana. Enjoy standing in the midst of all that color. Feel the yarn. No, really touch it. How is it going to feel against the wearer's skin? How is it going to drape? That wonderfully fuzzy stuff that you'd like to make a scarf out of? It's nylon. It will drape beautifully, wear not quite so beautifully, and be fairly warm. So knit it with a large open stitch that will allow the fuzzies somewhere to bloom. That ribbon yarn you'd love to use for a sweater? It's polyester, might even wash. But know that thin ribbon snags easily, so perhaps it should be knit for adults only, or anyway for someone who understands the concept of delicate fabric. How about the ribbon woven in cotton and rayon? Tough stuff. Whatever you make, the garment will probably grow, since neither fiber has give or memory. But it will be cool and comfortable.

Decisions, decisions, informed decisions. Nirvana.

A Note on Felting

Any 100 percent wool, or wool blended with other animal fibers (such as alpaca and mohair), will felt as long as it hasn't been treated to be washable—check the ball band. Use 100 percent animal fibers for your felted bag, hat, scarf, or jacket. If you're not sure about a particular yarn, make a swatch and try felting it to check the results. But that doesn't mean you can't get wild and crazy about what you stir in with wool for your project. Most synthetic fibers, excluding rayon, go through the felting hot-wash process unchanged.

Many novelty yarns—eyelash, ribbons, railroad yarns—are synthetic. In doubt? Felt a sample swatch.

Felted wool bag with synthetic fiber trim

Yarn

Reading Yarn Labels—What You Need to Know

Not only do yarn labels suggest gauge (see Gauge, page 88), they also give you other information about the yarn.

1 Fiber content (see Choosing Fibers, page 99).

2 Dye lot number. Manufacturers dye their yarn in batches, or lots. Because of human nature and the nature of fiber, each batch may be slightly different. This is particularly noticeable in white yarn. Make sure all the yarn for a given project has the same dye lot number on the labels. If it's just not possible to find enough skeins in the same dye lot in the yarn you covet, combine the different lots throughout, changing from one lot to

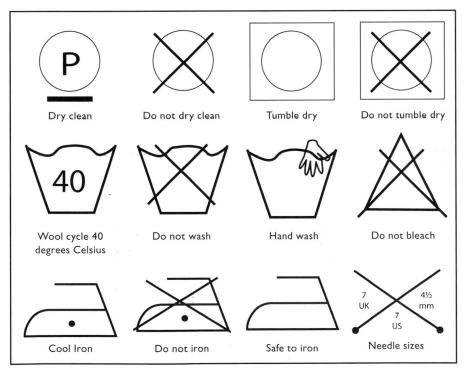

Yarn label symbols

another every few rows (see page 50). This blends the colors.

3 Care and cleaning instructions (see chart on page 103).

> Any time you mix two different fibers in one project, dry clean, no matter what it says on the yarn label.

4 Yardage. With this crucial bit of information, it's possible to figure out how many balls of yarn you need for a particular project. It's also possible to compare yarn value. If, say, one kind of bulky alpaca costs $6.50 for 50 yards and another costs $12 for 100 yards, the latter actually costs less.

How Much Yarn to Buy

If you're making the exact garment from the pattern in the exact yarn specified, knowing how much yarn to buy is easy—the pattern will probably tell you. But if you're substituting yarns, you'll need to figure out the yardage for your pattern.

Multiply the number of balls called for in the specified yarn by the number of yards per ball to find the total yardage. Divide the total yardage by the number of yards per ball of your chosen yarn to find out how many balls of your chosen yarn to buy.

However, always buy an extra ball or two of yarn. They're sometimes called "insurance skeins," and you buy them just in case . . .

- the pattern yardage is wrong—yep, it happens

- you knit more tightly than the pattern designer anticipated

- altering the pattern makes it bigger

- the yarn is discontinued before you finish the project

- the store runs out of your dye lot— if it's a popular yarn, this happens constantly

- your yarn is back-ordered for months

Reputable yarn stores allow unused, unopened insurance skeins to be returned for store credit, usually within three to six months of purchase and with your receipt.

Conclusion

*T*hings were getting out of hand in my office/studio: on every surface yarn, needles, patterns, sketches of pattern ideas, gauge swatches. Now that everything's nicely organized (for the moment), I realize that the place is a picture of risk-taking in action. All right, so physical risk-taking like skydiving or mountain climbing doesn't appeal to me. Instead, I'm willing to risk buying some sumptuous yarn to realize what's in my mind's eye. That hand-dyed laceweight mohair and matching bouclé in the knitting bag next to me? I'm knitting strips of each, playing with the notion of alternating them into a modular sweater. That cream Aran-weight yarn sitting right in front of the computer monitor is the beginning of a cabled sweater (think cables that look like leaves on the vine) that's knit to fit beginning with the center back section and continuing over the shoulders and down the front. Neither of these projects comes with a guarantee of success. The fun is in the experimentation.

Take a risk with your yarn. See what happens. If the result is unexpected, take pleasure in the possibilities. And if things go awry, you've got this book.

Acknowledgments

Knitters are lucky people because we can rely on each other for help. When I walked into Janet Avila's shop, String Theory Yarn Co., in Glen Ellyn, Illinois, and asked if I could teach a class on correcting mistakes, she said, "Sure, show me the syllabus." Then I told her that I had an ulterior motive—testing out my ideas on her customers for this book. Instead of being appalled she was delighted, and has helped constantly along the way. Thanks to her and all my students, including those at Three Bags Full yarn shop in Northbrook and owner Lynette Swanson. To Veronika, a.k.a. Dr. G, for asking the perfect diagnostic question. A special shout-out to Mary Beth Woodall, artist and knitter who asks the most wonderful questions, and who also let me test ideas, explanations, and parts of the book on her.

I've been blessed with a wonderful editor, Anne Merrow, who steered Knit Fix onto the right road and kept it there. Anne is fast becoming the Max Perkins of the knitting book set. Thanks to Betsy Armstrong, acquisitions editor at Interweave Press, for her patience while a journalist figured out how to be a book author. And to Interweave's art department, who created lovely illustrations out of knitting mistakes.

Knitters are adventurous people with a "let me try this" attitude toward the art. Over the years, strangers and relatives have shown me new techniques, which I'd then apply to my own knitting. Thanks to my father for his insight into color and to my mother for her advanced knowledge of sewing.

I want particularly to thank two people who have now passed out of our lives, my cousin Shirley Goldberg, and my father-in-law, Irving Kartus. Both were the kind of people who gave of themselves unstintingly. They listened to me, they laughed at and with me. Everyone should be so lucky to have a Shirley or an Irv in her life.

Above all, this book is for Jesse, my partner in all things.

The Basics of Knitting

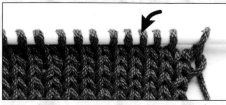

Knit stitch

Purl stitch

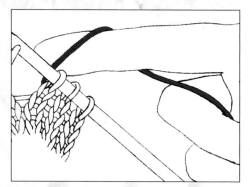

English tension

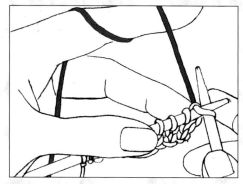

Continental tension

Working yarn

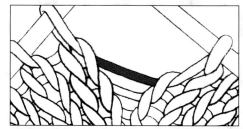

Running stitch

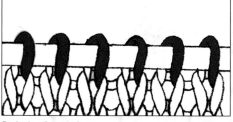

Right leg forward

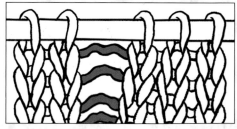

Dropped stitch ladder

Yarnover

A Guide to Common Errors

Accidental increases

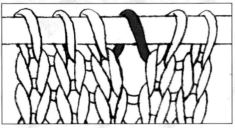

Yarnover

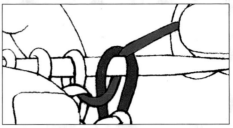

Knitting first stitch as two

Holes

Dropped stitch

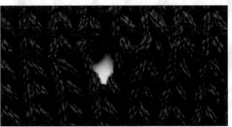

Yarnover hole

Other possible errors

Reverse direction

Twisted stitches

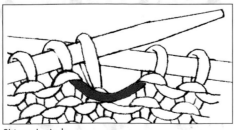

Skipped stitch

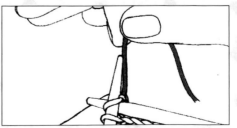

Yarn not sufficiently tensioned

Index

acrylic 99, 101–102
altering, 77–86
alpaca 99–100, 102
angora 99, 100; goats 100
animal fibers 99–100
armhole 32; easing in 69
assembly, garment 68–70

backward loop cast-on 55–56
ball band gauge 88–89
bamboo 99–101
bind-off, standard 65; purl
    65–66; ssk 67; ssp 67;
    elastic 67; tight 66; in
    pattern 66; for lace 67
blending dye lot color 50
blocking 73–74; lace 73
bound-off edges 77–79
brake needle 24
burying yarn tails 47
buttons, buying to fit 60
buttonholes 60

cable cast-on 52–53
cable needle 34, 36
cables, crossed incorrectly
    9–10; repairing, 36–38
camel hair 99
care, fabric 74, 103–104
cashmere 99–100
cast-off see bind-off
cast-on, backward loop
    55–56; cable 52–53; long-
    tail 54–55; removing; rib-
    bing 53; evenly 53 in the
    middle of a row 55–56;
    to work in the round 58;
    twisted 58
cast-on edges 80–82
chart symbols 42–43
charts 9, 40; reading 42–44
choosing fiber 99
circumference of yarn 88
clip fix, 80-82
color blending, dye lot 50
color 45–50; kinds of color
    knitting 45; changing col-
    ors, 45; repairing mistakes
    in 48–50; in intarsia 50
Continental method, holding
    yarn 12; tension 16–17,
    106; knit 13; purl 14;

defined 12
control unraveling stitches 24
control yarn 16 see also
    tension
cotton 74, 99–101
counting rows 40–41
counting stitches 8, 9, 39–41
cuff 77, 81

decreases, missed 32; ssk 40;
    k2tog 39; p2tog 39
drape 76, 83, 100–101
dropped stitches 22–23,
    33–35; in Fair Isle or
    intarsia 48–49; holes 107;
    ladder 106
dry clean 104
duplicate stitch 49–50
dye lots; 50, 103–104; blend-
    ing 50

ease, garment 93
easing in fabric 68–70
edges, cast-on 80–82; bound-
    off 77–79
elasticity, in yarn 99–101
Enchanted Forest sweater 98
English method, holding yarn
    12; tension 16–17, 106;
    knit 13, purl 14; defined
    12
errata 64
even cast-on 53
even stitches 73, see also
    tension

fabric care 103–104
fabric ease 68
Fair Isle defined, 45; repair-
    ing mistakes in 48–50
felting 102
fiber, animal 100; natural
    100–101; synthetic 101
fiber chart 99
fiber, choosing 99; yarn
    content 103
finishing 74; weaving in ends
    47
fit, garment 93–98

gaps, in Fair Isle 46; when
    joining in the round, 58;

when picking up and knit-
    ting 62; at gussets 63
garter stitch 8, 23
gauge 88–90; altering with
    97; swatch 89–91; in
    cables 89; suggested
    103–104
garment assembly 68–70
garment ease 93
grafting 71–73
gussets, altering with 83–84;
    in socks 63

hanging stitches 22, 23, 33
hem 77, 80, 81
holding yarn 16–17 see also
    tension
holes, accidental 30, 31;
    dropped stitch 107; on
    edges 62–63; reversed
    direction 28; in color knit-
    ting 45; yarnover 40
horizontal fixes 20–21

increase, yarnover 44
increases, accidental 107
insurance strips 104
intarsia 45; altering in 96

joining new colors 45–47
joining yarn 56–57
joining in the round 57–58
joins, seam 71–73

Kandinsky sweater 95
Karan, Donna 98
Kartus, Irving 4
Kitchener stitch 71–73
knit stitch 12, 13, 15, 106;
    saving dropped 22
knit two together (k2tog) 39
knit one stitch as two,
    accidental increase 31
knit up stitches see pick up
    and knit
ktbl (knit through back loop)
    27

labels, yarn 88–89; 103–104
lace, binding off 67; charts
    43–44
ladders, stitch 22, 23, 106

length, altering 77–82, 85–86, 95–98
length, fixing uneven 68–70
linen 99–101
live stitches, adding 61–63
long-tail cast-on 54–55
Lycra 101

magnetic board 9
magnetic strip 9
markers, stitch 8, 9
measuring for a garment 94
microfiber 101
mistakes in patterns 64; in yardage 104
mitred squares 61, 80
Möbius 58
modular knitting 61, 80
mohair 80, 99–100, 102

natural fiber 100–101
neck alterations 78–79
needle size 88
no stitch symbol in chart 43–44
novelty yarn 102
nylon 99, 101–102

patterns 40,
pattern revisions 94–98
pick up and knit, 61–63
picking up dropped knit stitches 22, dropped purl stitches 23: see also pick up and knit
ply 31
pockets, adding when finished 81–82
polyamid 99
polyester 99
purl stitch 12, 14, 15, 106; saving hanging 23
purl two together (p2tog) 39
ptbl (purl through back loop) 27

Radford, Leigh 95
rayon 73, 99–101
repeat 43, 96
repairing holes see holes
reversing direction, avoiding 28, 107
revising patterns 94–98
right leg forward 12, 106

round, working in 57–59
row marker 9
rows, counting 40–41; lengthen or shorten with 96
running stitch 32, 106

saving dropped knit stitches 22; purl stitches 23
seams, altering at 83–84
sewing machine 76, 85–87
silk 73, 74, 99–101
simple cast-on 55
size of garment 93–98
skipped stitches 29, 107
slanted stitches 30
sleeves, easing in 69 adjustment 85–86
slipknot 52
slipped stitches, at edge 62; see also skipped stitches
slip-slip-knit 40; bind-off 67
slip-slip-purl 40; bind-off 67
socks 34; casting on for 53; picking up stitches in 63
soy 99–101
split stitch 31
steam 73
stitch counter 41
stitch ladders 22, 23, 106
stitch markers, placing 8, 9
stitch mistakes, vertical fixes for 22–21
stitches, counting 8, 9, 39–41; dropped 33–35, 48–49, 107; duplicate 49–50; even 53; hanging 22; picking up 24, 61–63; unknitting 20–21; unraveling 24; reversing direction of 28; running 32; skipped 29, 107; slanted yarnover 30, 40; split 31; too few 33–35; too many 30–32; twisted 26–29, 107
stranding, 46–48; across back of work 46, 48; up side of work 47
stitches, narrow or widen with number of 97
swatches, gauge 88–91
synthetic fiber 101

Tencel 99–101
tension 16–17, 88, 106, 107 see also gauge
tight knitting 9
tinking see unknit
too few stitches 33–35
too many stitches 30–32
trading stitches 59
twisted stitches 12, 26–29, 107; avoiding 27
twisted cast-on 58

unknit, how to 21–20
unpurl 21
unraveling stitches 24

vertical fix for knit and purl 22–23, garter 23, on color 48, for dropped stitches 22–23, 33; for cables, 36

washing garment 74
weaving in yarn tails 47
weight of yarn 92
width, altering 85–86
wool 74, 99–102; Merino 100; Shetland 100
working in the round 28, 57–59
working yarn 8, 12, 106, 107; thrown over needle 31
wrap around needle for knit 13; for purl 14

yardage 104
yarn chart 99
yarn, color crossing 45–46; holding 16–17; how much to buy 104; joining 56–57; labels 103; working 8, 12, 106; running out of 55
yarnover, accidental 30; avoiding 31, 106; holes 107; on knit side 30, 40; on purl side 30, 40; increases 40, 43–44 in lace 44; working yarn position for, 44; buttonholes
yarn tails, weaving in 47; avoiding knitting with 55
yarn weights chart 92